Neil "Soapy" Castles

Neil "Soapy" Castles

Memoir of a Life in NASCAR and the Movies

Henry Neil "Soapy" Castles
with Perry Allen Wood

Foreword by Deb Williams

McFarland & Company, Inc., Publishers
Jefferson, North Carolina

ISBN (print) 978-1-4766-7628-9
ISBN (ebook) 978-1-4766-3504-0

Library of Congress cataloguing data are available

British Library cataloguing data are available

© 2019 Henry Neil Castles and Perry Allen Wood. All rights reserved

No part of this book may be reproduced or transmitted in any form or by any means, electronic or mechanical, including photocopying or recording, or by any information storage and retrieval system, without permission in writing from the publisher.

Front cover: In February of 1970, Neil Castles was one of Chrysler Corporation's "Winged Warriors" with his sleek Dodge Daytona seen during "Speed Weeks" at the Daytona International Speedway (*Neil Castles Family Collection*)

Printed in the United States of America

McFarland & Company, Inc., Publishers
Box 611, Jefferson, North Carolina 28640
www.mcfarlandpub.com

My life has been a long tough trip with more highs and lows than I can remember. I do know that without my grandparents and parents having such an incredible work ethic to pass on to me I could never have made it this far. There are so many people who helped me along the way and I hope I thanked them good enough in the book.

I'd like to dedicate this book and my life to my family. To Jean, who stood beside me all these years and raised three wonderful children and is still here today. She is the cement that has always kept us all together and always will. And to the kids, Susan, Donna, and Neil, Jr., for hanging in there through all the adventures and misadventures they experienced going from track to track and town to town during my racing days. Since then right up to this very moment all four of them and their families have stuck with me and I love them for doing it. This is not my book, it is *OUR* book. Thank you for making it possible.

Henry Neil Castles

Table of Contents

Acknowledgments by Perry Allen Wood	viii
Foreword by Deb Williams	1
Preface by Perry Allen Wood	3
ONE. A Beginning	7
TWO. Behind the Wheel and on the Gas	16
THREE. After Buddy	37
FOUR. Racing into the '60s	60
FIVE. Elvis Is in the Building	79
SIX. Inspections, Rescues, Wings and Protests	98
SEVEN. That Championship Feeling	113
EIGHT. Lights, Camera and Lots of Action	136
NINE. Taking on the Giant	160
TEN. Heading for the Checkered Flag	172
ELEVEN. Neil's Children Reflect	183
Index	189

Acknowledgments
by Perry Allen Wood

First and foremost I want to thank the entire Castles family for their tremendous cooperation in the writing of this book. Every interview appointment was kept and I was given total access to their albums, documents, hearts, and minds. From the start, daughters Susan and Donna and son Neil, Jr., added useful information, advice, and corrections. Neil's wife Jean sat in on every interview and added needed clarification, often when Neil was unsure of a recollection as much as 60 years old. The cooperation shown with my prying into the Castles family's history, and Neil's discussing things I knew he would rather not remember, heightens the responsibility to do their emotional investments justice. Thank you from the bottom of my heart.

Thanks are due once again to my bosses at Wells Fargo Bank Financial Crimes Investigations. Matt Reinbeck and David Burton never failed to cooperate with me when I needed a day off here, half a day there, and frequent lunch hours skipped so I could leave the office in Charlotte early and interview Neil, who conveniently lives on my way home to Spartanburg.

Last and never least is my family, who can be seen growing up in the acknowledgments of each book. This time, I give my heartfelt appreciation and love to Yaneth, my wife of 25 years. Little Hannah, whom I thanked in 2007, is a beautiful young woman now enrolled at the University of South Carolina. And Jake, the little boy who trudged around in the woods with me as I was searching for those *Silent Speedways of the Carolinas* in 2007, is married and on his first tour of duty in Okinawa with the "America's Battalion," the 2nd Battalion 8th Marines. My deepest thanks to all of you for letting me keep writing books while doing your own things, which makes me prouder than you all can imagine.

Foreword
by Deb Williams

To many race fans, Neil Castles was an independent in NASCAR's premier series who seemed to always play second fiddle to those teams that either were factory backed or possessed a high-profile sponsor. However, the man who acquired the nickname "Soapy" during his Soap Box Derby days was so much more.

A Charlotte, North Carolina, native, Neil Castles was a champion, capturing the 1972 NASCAR Grand National East Series title. That year he collected two victories and 20 top-10 finishes. In two years in that series, he led 423 laps in 29 races, possessed an average finish of 7.2 and never placed lower than second in the standings.

Neil Castles also competed in the sanctioning body's Convertible Series, posting six top-10 finishes in 55 races from 1957 through 1959.

However, it was the 19 years that Neil Castles spent in NASCAR's premier series when he became a household name with grassroots race fans. Making his debut on the circuit in 1957 in Columbia, South Carolina, Castles began running the majority of the races on the arduous schedule in 1964. He missed only two events in 1969, when the schedule consisted of 54 races. That was the year he produced a fourth-place finish in the driver standings, the best of his career on the prestigious circuit. Castles also won two qualifying races during that time, one for the Southern 500 at Darlington, South Carolina, in 1967, and the other in 1969 for the Carolina 500 at Rockingham, North Carolina. Before retiring in 1976, Castles competed in 498 races, recording 51 top-five and 178 top-10 finishes. He also led 70 of the 90,403 laps he completed.

Unknown to many outside of racing was Castles' other business endeavor. When he wasn't racing in NASCAR, his driving talents were quite popular in Hollywood. He handled the driving duties for Elvis Presley in the movie *Speedway*. Castles also was a stunt driver in six other movies: *Thunder*

Foreword by Deb Williams

Road, which was filmed in Asheville, North Carolina; *The Last American Hero*, filmed in North Carolina and Virginia; *Hot Summer in Barefoot County*; *Greased Lightning*; *Six Pack* and *What Comes Around*. Neil Castles also acted in a television series and two movies, served as a technical advisor for others, and worked in the transportation department for eight movies and one TV series. He was involved in countless projects for which he got no credits at all.

Perhaps, though, it's Neil Castles' philosophy that led him to experience one of racing's most intriguing stories. He believed that something odd will happen every day. And as his memoir shows, it did.

Deb Williams is an award-winning contributor to espnW.com and senior writer for RacinToday.com. Among her past positions, she was the editor of *NASCAR Winston Cup Scene* for ten years, managing editor of *GT Motorsports*, and an instructor in Southern Motorsports at Appalachian State University.

Preface
by Perry Allen Wood

I first approached Neil Castles about working together to write his life story after meeting him at an event at the old Hillsborough Speedway in September 2007. Here was the quintessential hard-nosed, independent stock car racer of the 1950s through the mid–1970s, much as I remembered him back at Columbia Speedway for that first paved 100-mile Grand National in 1971. Well respected as both a racer and a Hollywood stunt man, he had performed the crashes in one of my all-time favorite movies, *Thunder in Carolina*, and I remembered his having a camera mounted on the back of his 1965 Dodge number 06 during the 1967 World 600 for Elvis Presley's flick *Speedway*

Neil's unique story as an independent racer and Hollywood stunt man would make a great book, I told him. He seemed receptive to the idea. At another event the following weekend, Neil and his lovely wife Jean indicated that they were very much interested in a book project, but that there was a whole lot more than just racing and stunting to Neil Castles. They explained a part to Neil's life that might dwarf the rest of the story, wanting to give me a chance to bail out if I chose to. They had been tied up in litigation for many years with corporate super-giant Exxon over petroleum leakage at a tank farm in the Paw Creek area of northwest Mecklenburg County, North Carolina. They explained that this contamination of the ground and water had effectively diseased an entire community, costing many of their neighbors' lives, and Neil Castles his left eye and a good bit of skull surrounding it. The bottom line was that this ordeal was a major part of Neil's life and he would want to recount it in the book. I never flinched at including his full story, and we shook hands in agreement.

In a letter dated October 10, 2007, I outlined my thoughts about the book in more detail. The following month, at their invitation, I visited Jean and Neil Castles at their gorgeous home at the Pine Island Country Club golf course northwest of Charlotte. In the course of a most enjoyable afternoon

Preface by Perry Allen Wood

I listened to Neil's stories, looked at his huge collection of racing artifacts and photographs, and learned much more about the effects of the groundwater contamination, Neil's resulting illness and the legal battle with Exxon. As we said our goodbyes we agreed that after the holidays, Neil and I would start on the book in early January 2008.

Over the next few months I wrote Neil letters and spoke to Jean and him once at an event, but he did not reply to my letters or phone messages. Eventually I concluded that he had developed cold feet because of the Exxon angle. As years passed and I completed other books, I always held out hope that someday Neil and I would write that book. I ran into Jean and Neil several times and always asked Neil when we were going to write the book. Then on October 21, 2017, when Greg Moore and I attended the Old Timers Racing Association awards ceremony at Richard Childress's racing complex in Welcome, North Carolina, in walked Jean, Neil, and Neil Castles, Jr., whom I had never met. We all shook hands, exchanged pleasantries, and Greg and I were introduced to Neil, Jr. He is actively involved in movie making, working on a set in Atlanta at the time.

Right on cue I blurted out, "Neil, when are we going to write that book?" To my great surprise he answered, "Let's go!" In my shock and joy I confirmed that he wanted to proceed with the writing, and our collaboration began, with the result that you are now holding.

It has been a pleasure and an honor to do my part in setting down the story of such a remarkable life in print. Here is a man who fought in the middle of the pack for years risking his life every lap just as much as Fireball Roberts, Joe Weatherly, or Tiny Lund did, and they died in the process. Here's a man who voluntarily drove cars at high speeds, purposely crashing them, often accompanied by fire, for the entertainment of moviegoers. Here's a man who took on one of the largest companies in the world and won. And here's a man who proudly perseveres in spite of a disfiguring disease and the loss of an eye. A photograph from the 1966 World 600 speaks volumes about Neil Castles, in my mind. Neil was piloting one of Buck Baker's under-funded, under-powered Oldsmobiles with no realistic chance of winning from 37th position in a starting field of 44. At some point midway through the 400-lap ordeal, the windshield completely blew out of the racer at well over 130 miles per hour. Neil Castles pitted, took off his helmet, wrapped a white towel around his face except for his goggled eyes, put his headgear back on, and took to the asphalt once again. A black and white photograph shows Neil Castles peering straight ahead, helmet strapped on to hold the towel covering his face in place, hands on the wheel, and the windshield missing. Today, NASCAR would never permit that, even if some driver would consider trying it. But Neil Castles did. And not only did he finish—Neil Castles rumbled to the checkers in fifth place! That's the nature of this man who knows danger all too well. A man who for more than half a century has overpowered danger every single time.

I hope you enjoy the story of one courageous man: Henry Neil "Soapy" Castles.

One

A Beginning

I was born in Marion, North Carolina, on October 1, 1934, on my daddy's birthday. He was Donald Jackson Castles and mother was Elizabeth Rucker Castles. On the next page is a picture of my parents and my Daddy is carrying a baby, a little boy, their first child. He was born with an enlarged liver and they took him to Spartanburg to that major hospital down there back then and he only lived a short amount of time. When he passed away, Mother and Daddy went down there and brought him back to her mother's house which was in Gilkey, North Carolina, halfway between Rutherfordton and Marion. They're walking up the walk into the house with the baby when they come back from the hospital. Daddy is carrying the baby. He carried the baby on his lap back from Spartanburg. They made the funeral arrangements and had the baby buried at Mountain Creek Baptist Church on 221 going into Rutherfordton on the left. I had no other brothers and sisters. That was the only one. Mother and Daddy are both buried there and I've got a lot of grandmothers and grandfathers, aunts and uncles buried there. That's the beginning.

Those grandparents were very much involved in the community, knew what was needed to make money, and moved to wherever the action was. The whole family were true mountain entrepreneurs.

My granddaddy, J. N. Castles, run the railroad depot in Thermal City, North Carolina. That's on 221 going to Marion, where they think they found gold, and all them people are down in that hole digging for it. He was the depot agent. My granddaddy hired all the people up there to cut wood because they had to have wood to run the train. He had a pipeline put in for mountain water from the top of the mountain behind there down to a big water tank so when the train come in they'd fill it up with water and load it with wood, then go on to Charlotte. Grandpa built a big hotel behind the railroad depot. So a train came in every week and all the people on the train stayed at the hotel on Friday or Saturday night until the train got watered up and serviced to leave the next day. Daddy went to school and become a telegraph operator and operated it for the railroad. His brother run the general store. Grandpa built the general store there on Main Street. The post office is still there. My grandmother ran the post office. She was the postal agent. So Grandma was running the post office, Uncle Ed running the general store, Daddy was the telegraph operator, and Grandpa run the railroad depot.

Going up 221 there's a big valley on the right-hand side down through there, a pasture, and on the other side of the road a big three-story white house stood on the shoulder. That was the first house Grandpa built. Well, they decided to move the train from Thermal City to Union Mills. So Grandpa went to Union Mills and built him a big house right there at the railroad station. The whole family moved to Union Mills and run those same jobs there for a long time. There's a lot of history there for the Castles family.

Neil's father Donald Jackson Castles and mother Elizabeth Rooker Castles bring his deceased newborn brother home from the Spartanburg hospital on May 25, 1929 (Neil Castles Family Collection).

Neil was on the move with his family for most of his early childhood due to his parents' jobs. He bounced around the family early on, staying with first one relative and then another.

My daddy was a barber after he was a telegraph operator, and my mother was a school teacher, and we moved to Spruce Pine, North Carolina. They offered him a big job up there on some kind of project. Then they moved to

One. A Beginning

The hotel Neil's grandfather J. N. Castles built behind the railroad station at Thermal City, North Carolina, is bustling with travelers for the train to Charlotte circa 1910 (Neil Castles Family Collection).

Lenoir and Daddy took a job in a big barber shop on the square. We stayed there and I started to school in Lenoir in the first grade. Then we moved to Charlotte. I attended school there in the Wilmore section, then in Dilworth, then they put some of us on the bus to go to Derita. I went to a half a dozen different schools. I stayed in Charlotte with Mother and Daddy. My aunt, who lived on a farm in Gilkey with her mother and daddy, taught school up there at Green Hill for 21 years in the first and second grades. So I went up and stayed with my granddaddy and grandma and went to school in Green Hill with my aunt through the second grade. Then I moved back to Charlotte and went to school in Wilmore through the fourth grade.

We bought a house on Merriman Avenue in Wilmore in Charlotte. From the back door of the house you just crossed the alley where the garbage trucks ran and went right straight into the church. I went to church there quite a while and was in the Boy Scouts for several years. I floated back and forth between there and Grandma's because Daddy was drafted into the Army.

They wanted telegraph operators. Mother being a school teacher, they put her to work at the quartermaster depot out there on Graham Street in Charlotte as a bean counter. That's where they recycled all the uniforms that came back from the Second World War.

On the end of those big long buildings they had fenced in a large amount of German prisoners that they'd brought in from overseas. They had them sorting uniforms and stuff. Mother worked there for quite a few years. While Daddy was down at Fort Bragg, he got pneumonia and they discharged him due to his health situation. He only stayed in the Army a year or so. Anyway, he was there until they run him off and he came back to Charlotte and went to work in a barber shop.

Neil joined the work force, making good use of his bicycle. He also made a major connection that charted the course of his life. It is more important than anything else.

I had a bicycle, naturally, and got a job delivering prescriptions for a pharmacy over in Dilworth in the evening after school. Well, that was sort of up and down, so I got a paper route for the evening paper. I had a route manager drop off the papers and we'd settle up the money on Saturday. The last newspaper I dropped off every evening at dark was at Shuman and Thompson's Garage at 325 Lincoln Street in Charlotte. That was Buddy Shuman and Willie Thompson that built racecars, many racecars. Well, I got fascinated with those racecars and they were building some pretty fast ones. That interested me. I guess I was in the fifth or sixth grade, so this had to be about 1946 or so.

Henry Neil Castles bounced from school to school before settling in Charlotte, North Carolina, to deliver newspapers and race Soap Box Derby cars circa 1942 (Neil Castles Family Collection).

One. A Beginning

I got to hanging around there in the evenings after I dropped off my last papers. One night Willie said, "If you ain't got nothing to do, boy, help me clean this shop up." So I started helping him clean up the shop in the evenings after I finished delivering my papers. That got to be a full-time thing. As soon as I got the last paper delivered, I flew in there and picked up the tools and I knew where they went. I worked around that shop for a long time helping out.

They were building '39 and '40 model racecars. Buddy had two brand-new cars built. Buddy was the driver and would let somebody drive the second car if he wanted to. A lot of times Fireball Roberts drove one of the cars and I was just fascinated with them. When I wasn't old enough, Buddy had a '40 Ford van and we put tires, jacks, tools, and spares in the back to have at the racetrack. Mary Bruner and Roby Combs' wife from Shelby handled the NASCAR [National Association for Stock Car Auto Racing] pits, the payoff, and everything.

But when you drove up to go in, you had to buy a NASCAR pit pass. Well, I wasn't old enough to even think about a pit pass. So Buddy used to

Best friend Fireball Roberts, left, with boss and mentor Buddy Shuman, right, with a Shuman and Thompson Garage modified Ford at an unidentified dirt track about 1948 (Neil Castles Family Collection).

Neil "Soapy" Castles

stand me down between them tires and we'd go right on in the pits. When things got up to working like getting the tires and stuff unloaded, I'd get out and start helping, but I'd stay close to the van. Another first in my life was getting in and out of the pits without getting caught.

As Neil Castles became more heavily involved in auto racing as just a kid, yet another event occurred that is reflected in his life every single day.

This boy that lived behind us in Dilworth, his daddy had a woodworking shop and they were building him a Soap Box Derby car. Well, I decided I wanted to build me one. So I got out and started hunting a sponsor. Buddy said, "You get you a sponsor to pay for the wheels and I'll help you." So I got a sponsor, Swinson's Food Products, and Buddy helped me with it.

From the shop up there down to where we lived was a pretty good jump right straight down the hill. You get down the hill and you could turn to get to our house. Well, I had that Soap Box Derby car and I'd been to the Soap Box Derby race with it and I'd push it up the hill. Well, there was a guy that lived right around the corner from me named Dippo Kelly. He had a Model A. He said, "Neil, just grab a rope there and hook it to the back bumper and when we get to the Wilmore Food Store, you just turn loose of the rope and go on down to the house and I'll see you." So I went down Cliftwood at a pretty good rate of speed behind that Model A and I saw I wasn't going to be able to make that turn, so I just went on down to Wilmore School and run up the bank into the school parking lot to the ball field.

By the time I got stopped at the ball field, the police were standing there waiting on me. He said, "I'll tell you what. We're going to let you push that Soap Box Derby back home because you ain't going to have it in the road no more. Do you know how fast you were going? You passed us." They got on me about having that Soap Box Derby in the road running so fast. That policeman didn't actually see that Model A pulling me. I came out from behind that Model A and I passed him. So me and the Soap Box Derby got back home.

The police went to the barber shop and got my daddy and took him out and had a little talk with him and told him, "That Soap Box Derby ain't coming out of the yard, so you go home and fix it." So that's where I got that nickname from people kidding me about that fast Soap Box Derby. All them boys at Shuman's shop and down at the beer joint knew that the police got me in that Soap Box Derby going down that hill. So Buddy Shuman started calling me "Soapy." They also called me "Soap."

One. A Beginning

Anointed with a nickname from one of the top local racers of the day, Soapy Castles had arrived on the scene, and the racing got more serious as far as he was concerned. Shuman and Thompson made sure Neil looked like he was part of it. And modifieds were not the only cars to roll in and out of the Shuman and Thompson shop.

While I stayed there and helped with them old cars and stuff, Buddy ordered me uniforms like he and Willie had. So now I've become part of a big racing team. We used to go to Strawberry Hill, which was a big dirt track in Richmond, Virginia, that Paul Sawyer had back then.

In the meantime they were also building some moonshine cars and this was in 1950 because they had a brand new '50 Ford coupe. I would have been 16 years old by now. We built the cars. We never delivered any moonshine. But from out of town they would come to Shuman to build them a better car. We built a lot of '40 Fords and a State Highway Patrolman came to them to build a Highway Patrol car. It was just one patrolman and he wanted a car as fast as he could get it. He was tired of getting outrun so he come over there to Shuman. He wanted a price on what it would take to do this, this, and this to his car. Buddy said, "Well, I'm in that business so we'll just fix it." We did!

When that car was finished, we took it out behind the airport to see how fast it would run. We had an old man that we'd take the cars to over by the airport to see if the speedometers were calibrated where they should be. He owned two sprint cars. Buddy drove one of the sprint cars and Herman Owens lived behind him in another house and Herman drove the other one. This wasn't NASCAR, this was Triple A [AAA, or the American Automobile Association]. We were running short tracks and the modifieds everywhere.

Buddy and Willie took a Cadillac engine and put it in that '50 Ford coupe. With 32 cases of liquor in it you could spin both rear tires at a hundred miles an hour. That become what they called "The Fordillac." That name was created at Shuman's and Thompson's putting Cadillac engines in Fords. That's how I got tied up in racing.

From some very hard racing and a growing accumulation of hardware from across the Southeast at Shuman's Garage, the suits from Detroit decided to help. As Neil's knowledge of racing increased as well as his expertise as a mechanic, he became an asset to the shop and started getting loaned out for other duties. And new lifelong associations were born.

Neil "Soapy" Castles

In 1951 we got brand-new Fords from Ford Motor Company. They had three of them and they gave them to Buddy. They said, "You pick who you want in the other two and you pick the one you want." We went to the Ford dealership in Pineville, North Carolina, and picked them out: one six-cylinder business coupe and two Police Interceptors. We brought them to the shop and started measuring what we needed to change, roll bars, and some things we thought we might could cheat on a little bit. Buddy wanted that six-cylinder because that was a flathead and we could deal with it. The other two we didn't know what we were going to do with them. So Ford sent two drivers and put Speedy Thompson in one and Fireball in the other. We ran that six-cylinder at Darlington in 1951 and Buddy drove it. Ford was sponsoring that.

Buddy Shuman stands behind Herman Owens at the wheel of his AAA midget in 1949 in Charlotte, North Carolina. Owens taught Neil how to drive a midget and bought him his first one (Neil Castles Family Collection).

The record shows that on September 3, 1951, in the largest field of cars to ever start a Grand National race, Buddy Shuman finished an incredible third in a 1951 six-cylinder flathead Ford number 17. They obviously knew what they were doing with them. Fireball brought one of the other Fords home fifth with no listing of Speedy in the records.

We put a Cadillac engine in an old Chevrolet for Bob Colvin. His brother Leland Colvin lived in Camden, South Carolina, and he kept up a racecar. Bob Colvin owned and operated the Darlington Raceway. Leland was in charge of all the peanuts and tobacco that was raised in that part of South Carolina. Bob and Leland had big tobacco warehouses in Darlington. Any-

One. A Beginning

body that had any tobacco or peanuts had to go through those tobacco warehouses to deal with the government. The government controlled the tobacco or peanuts. They had a big responsibility with all that tobacco and stuff, and Leland was still pretty well into racing. He'd get a new car every year.

On May 10, 1952, Neil witnessed a car he had worked on narrowly miss winning the 200-mile NASCAR Speedway Division race at Darlington. This was NASCAR's answer to the AAA's Big Car or Indianapolis Car Divisions. The races were fast and exciting, but the series only lasted one season. Leland Colvin's car with Speedy Thompson was on the pole.

At Darlington, that Ford Speedy Thompson was driving was leading with three laps to go and broke a drive shaft. The car sat in the back of the shop at Leland's and I wanted that car and told Leland. Well, Bondy Long, the guy with all the DuPont money from Camden, bought that car and made a dragster out of it and it didn't run. So they trashed it and nobody ever knew where it went.

The record shows that Speedy actually led frequently that day and was out front with 47 of the 160 laps to go when indeed the drive shaft broke for a disappointing 15th place as champion-to-be Buck Baker took the checkers.

By his late teens in the early 1950s, Neil Castles had set aside the books, and schoolhouse learning was over. He was deeply involved in both open wheel and modified stock car racing with a highly respected team and was developing relationships with individuals who were in the mainstream of the sport. It was inevitable that his role within the sport would soon expand.

Two

Behind the Wheel and On the Gas

In the late 1940s and early 1950s, Neil was in his teens, and a boy riding a bike quickly gave way to other forms of transportation, much faster, and much more dangerous. Racing was happening on multiple fronts for Neil, wheeling the dangerous midgets, sprints, and modifieds. He was becoming a racer with either wrenches or steering wheels in his hands, whether he got credit for it or not. With the events of November 1955, Neil Castles became a man.

The first thing that happened was Shuman carried me down there and got me my South Carolina driver's license. It didn't make a damn how old I was, we just went in, they signed me up, and I had a South Carolina driver's license. That way I could run up and down the road with no problem. I didn't have a North Carolina license yet because there was a year difference in age between the states of when you could get your license. You could get licensed a year younger in South Carolina than you could in North Carolina.

Herman Owens that drove the other sprint car when Shuman drove had a couple of midgets. I was fascinated with the midgets. Waco Dye bought a midget. He owned D.B. Dye Bolt Company and drove the car two or three races. He let Bob Harkey drive it. Bob Harkey had a dirt car he was running over at King's Mountain a lot and he wanted to run that midget of Waco's. Harkey ended up driving in the Indianapolis 500 several times.

Well, Herman was racing the sprints with Buddy and talked to me about it. So I went to Atlanta and bought a midget and Herman paid for it. I brought it back to the shop and me and Waco had two midgets in the shop. We rigged up a double-decker trailer where we could put one on top of the other one and haul them.

The biggest engines we had were Cushman motorcycle engines. During the war, the Army had hundreds of Cushman motorcycles, three-wheelers with boxes on the front of them, which they used to deliver stuff around the

Two. Behind the Wheel and on the Gas

bases and everywhere. So we could buy Cushman engines off those old Army vehicles and get whatever we needed from the people that were handling Cushman motor scooters. And the people that were handling them were also handling Harley Davidsons and Indians. We kind of graduated into that department, but I never raced a motorcycle.

About everybody had Cushman engines on those little old cars. We'd win a heat race, a consolation race, get a second or third or whatever we could get, and go. It didn't pay anything to amount to nothing. We just wanted to race. Then we'd go to Norfolk, Strawberry Hill, any races that were coming up.

It was going to happen sooner or later, so sooner was probably best. It is inherent to the sport of auto racing that you are going to crash and see crashes, and as a result, see and experience things that you wish you had not. Neil was involved at a time when safety was no more than an afterthought to speed. Death was a weekly occurrence and absolutely accepted. It got started for Neil in his midget and he was lucky.

I crashed that midget at Greasy Corners in Norfolk, Virginia, and flipped it five or six times through a pile of railroad crossties they had for a fence.

All alone for the moment, teenager Neil Castles is at the wheel of his first midget in the pits at an unknown racetrack circa 1950 (Neil Castles Family Collection).

That ended that midget. I was going down the backstretch and the radius rod on the right front broke and it dug into the racetrack and when it did, it shot me up into the whitewashed fence of big boards and old crossties. I got up in those crossties and it flipped. Waco and Bob Harkey was out there in the infield with that other car. They came running across the infield to see if I got hurt and fell into a gulley and liked to broke their necks. I got out from under the car and brushed off my britches, we loaded the car up, and brought that midget home. There wasn't anything left of it.

I had a few scratches, but the helmet I had on was the first helmet that Fireball ever had. He gave it to me when he was driving that car for Leland and I had my name painted across the front. When I wrecked that midget, it busted it [the helmet] into several pieces hitting those railroad ties. When I got home I put it in a box and laid it up on the closet shelf. So I ran the midgets for a good while. About this time, I drove a dirt car over in King's Mountain, North Carolina. So I graduated from the Soap Box Derby to home-made midgets around Charlotte to manufactured midgets to modifieds.

Rescuers and spectators rush to the scene as Neil Castles is pulled from beneath a violent midget crash at Greasy Corners Speedway in Norfolk, Virginia, in 1952 (Neil Castles Family Collection).

Two. Behind the Wheel and on the Gas

The story of Neil's first helmet is a tale that lives on to this day.

The helmet Fireball gave me was the first helmet I ever had. The reason I had it was because Fireball got a new one. We were in Roy Jones's shop over there at the airport and Fireball picked that helmet up and took a pair of tin snips and trimmed some off the bill. He just trimmed it down. He didn't like it. Well, we were in Charlotte and we were going to Daytona and he was in the back seat asleep. He wouldn't drive across the street if he could get to the back seat. Anyway, he got that new helmet and give me the old one. I used it. It was the only helmet I had.

After Jean and I got married, she got that box down out of the closet and wanted to know what that thing was. She got to looking at it and since the pieces were there, Jean and Mother got it on the table and glued it back together. After they glued it back together you couldn't tell it, and I started using it again for years. Nobody inspected helmets back then. They didn't care what you used. Nobody knew what you had on your head. I had one of

The helmet Fireball Roberts gave Neil as it looks today, resting in Neil's and Jean's basement. Close examination reveals Fireball's trimming of the bill and Jean's repair job (Perry Allen Wood Racing Archives).

those old Cromwell helmets with the leather sides, but I don't know what happened to it. I've got eight helmets up at Alex Beam's museum.

Continuing to log laps in the midget, sprints, and modifieds, one thing was for sure. Neil Castles knew what he liked to race on. It was a natural.

I thought when they first put asphalt down they'd ruined racing forever. I figured that was the end of it because I had started with them old midgets and sprint cars and if you couldn't go backwards through the corner you weren't going nowhere. I enjoyed the dirt tracks better. I never had any asphalt tires. Never had no dealings with them. Dirt tires we'd been running with for years. We'd take them to the tire store and hone off of them. Shave the edges and mold them to run different racetracks. So I was a hell of a lot further ahead with dirt than I was with asphalt. It was a transition from dirt to asphalt. The best racetrack I liked was Langhorne, Pennsylvania. It was just a big circle. You could drive it just like you could a sprint car. I remember Spartanburg very well, but that was in a stock car. Racing is racing. I believed in running down in the corner and as it gets looser, let it slide. If you could pass somebody on the inside going in, you could beat them off the corner. Anytime you could beat a car from the center of the corner to the center of the backstretch, you were gone.

Racecar driving was happening for Neil "Soapy" Castles, but the pay was minute. He depended on his work in the shop and parents just to get by.

I didn't get a paycheck from the garage. I didn't have any real source of income. Anything I needed, Buddy would buy. Buddy had a desk and had all the money in a drawer. That was to buy drinks and cookies and stuff for the shop. There wasn't anybody in the shop except Buddy, Willie, and me, and every once in a while we had a helper. Also, I was still living at home with Mother and Daddy so I didn't really need anything. Daddy was still a barber. I didn't graduate from high school. I finished the tenth or eleventh grade and went to working fulltime at Shuman's.

I was working on the racecars and going from racetrack to racetrack with those old midgets. I ran a lot of sprint cars, too. I was involved in the sprint car crash in Shelby, North Carolina, when Charlie Miller got killed in September of 1955. I graduated out of that into one of those '39 Ford coupes I ran at King's Mountain for a while. So did Bill Widenhouse from Midland, North Carolina. He drove dirt cars and his daddy owned a big sawmill.

Two. Behind the Wheel and on the Gas

Bill came to Shuman's every week with a truckload of slabs that he sold to people for firewood. Shuman nicknamed him "Slabs." Shuman was good at nicknames. He'd sell a truckload of slabs and come back to Shuman's and buy a set of Edelbrock heads or a carburetor and a manifold. He was building a car down at Midland for himself. Speedy Thompson, Jimmy Thompson, and old man Bruce Thompson lived in Monroe, North Carolina. Slabs got old man Bruce to do his welding for him. Tommy Boger drove old man Thompson's car and Speedy and Jimmy started building their own.

Neil experienced a great loss while his racing career was finding its legs. A pitiful episode took place in Norfolk, Virginia.

Daddy went to Norfolk to work, as a barber, I don't remember what year, and had setback [a relapse] of that pneumonia. They took him to a military hospital and they called Mother and wanted his papers from where he had pneumonia when he was in the Army. Well, she didn't have them. I was only a kid about 17 years old and I didn't know where they were either. They could have given him two shots of penicillin and cured it right on the spot. But since they couldn't find his service records, they couldn't help him. Mother called her aunt and uncle and me and Uncle Dave all went to the hospital in Norfolk. They had him on a bed rolled out in the hallway. I walked up to the bed and put my hand on his hand and said, "Well, Dad, I'm here." He looked at me and said, "That's good," and he died. He died right out in the hallway of that Norfolk hospital.

It was tough as hell for Neil to see his father go that way, but at least he was there at the end. His father was very sadly gone and it was time to get back to his other family, his growing racing family. Neil Castles was toughening up, and it would get tougher as death reared its horrible head occasionally for the next 50 years. As Neil would find out over and over time after time after being brushed by death in the years to come, life goes on and so must he. Thankfully, there was little time to dwell on the unpleasant as his services were needed elsewhere.

Neil was learning his trade from the best possible teachers; the now legendary Buddy Shuman and William Thompson were top of the line in the mechanics of auto racing. Shuman and Thompson University was a great place to learn and grow. There was only one person who ever earned a degree there and it was a master's: Henry Neil "Soapy" Castles.

Neil "Soapy" Castles

I learned to build Ford transmissions at Shuman's. Back when we were building moonshine cars, you could take a Ford transmission and change the main drive gear, the second slide gear, and a reverse idle gear, and mix them with standard Ford transmissions. You could run up to 100 miles an hour in second gear, jerk it back into high gear, and let it spin the tires. That was just by putting that extra high gear in second. You'd start off in first, wind it up, shift into second, and by the time you brought it back to high gear you were running 120 miles an hour.

One modified dirt track night, Neil found himself subbing for a future Hall of Famer. He could handle it and the boss knew it.

When we were at the racetracks we had two cars. We were in Greenwood, South Carolina, with the modified and Fireball was driving. They got Fireball to come to the telephone and he found out his wife was sick. So he jumped in a car and left for Daytona immediately. I got on the phone and called Leland and told him what had happened with Fireball and he said, "I know it. Go on and drive Fireball's car. Then hook to it and bring it on back." They were going to have some fun with me because that car of Leland's and Fireball's was fast. They put me up front in the first heat race. I didn't wait for them to start the race. I got halfway between three and four and stuck my foot in it and I was gone. I ran it in the heat race and I ran it in the main race, but I don't know where I finished. Everybody that had a racecar was there that night.

Neil was getting so good at everything related to auto racing, Shuman and Thompson started farming him out. It led to more education and skills.

Leland and them came up there to Charlotte and they were building a new racecar for Darlington. They told Buddy that they'd like me to come to Camden and help them build the car. They had a shop in the back of a Texaco station where they had the racecars. So me and Fireball used to haul loads of tobacco to R.J. Reynolds every week up in Winston-Salem. I had a '46 Ford tractor with a flatbed trailer. I took an Oldsmobile race engine we had and put it in that tractor. I could pretty much rule the roost going from Camden to R.J. Reynolds.

I went to Camden and helped build the racecar and Fireball Roberts drove it. I had a room in Leland's house and stayed there. Fireball lived there

Two. Behind the Wheel and on the Gas

Moving on up the ladder of auto racing, Neil Castles stands with his modified Ford outside owner Leland Colvin's shop in Camden, South Carolina, about 1954 (Neil Castles Family Collection).

part of the time. Leland had two or three spare bedrooms and we'd just come and go. Leland put me on the payroll. When I was living there in '53 or '54, Buck Baker put his boy Buddy in that military school there in Camden. Buck wanted Margaret to go with him to the races. So they shipped Buddy down there to that military school with me just around the corner.

Leland got a new car in 1953 from Oldsmobile. That was the car that Fireball sat on the pole with at Darlington and at 30-something laps blew a right front tire and knocked the wall down. But we fixed it. Later at Raleigh in 1954, we were pitting next to Speedy Thompson and I did a commercial for Union Oil. I poured a can of Union Oil into the car for a commercial for them.

The record shows that on September 7, 1953, Fireball Roberts started Leland Colvin's 1953 Oldsmobile number 11 in sixth place and led the Southern

Neil Castles, left, and an unidentified company representative filmed a Pure Oil commercial with Fireball Roberts' Oldsmobile at Raleigh Speedway in 1953 (Neil Castles Family Collection).

500 for 41 laps until he crashed. It officially says "A frame," but that is likely what broke on the car to cause the accident.

From Shuman's Garage to Leland Colvin's shop, Neil found himself working even further south in a building full of legends. The experiences were priceless.

Me and Red Vogt were good friends and Red was in charge of the cars at Fish Carburetor in Daytona Beach, Florida. Fireball lived in Daytona and we were running back and forth between Shuman's and Daytona Beach over at Fish Carburetor. Fireball was driving that M-1 that Fish built. They had M-1, 2, 3, 4 and M-5 all built in an old fire station in Monroe. The old building

Two. Behind the Wheel and on the Gas

didn't even have a decent roof on it. It leaked. Me and Speedy built that car and went to Daytona and all the cars finished in the top five or six. We had a Buick Skylark and old man Fish wanted that M and a number on there.

I worked in Daytona for Fish with Ray Fox and Fireball building flathead engines. Red Vogt was building the engines and I was cleaning up pistons and fitting bearings. Next when we got it built we put it on the dyno. We had a pretty good homemade dyno and checked a lot of engines for other teams. Every time we'd check one of those Fish Carburetors, if it wouldn't come up to snuff, we'd just open the back door and throw it in the river. The building backed up to the Halifax River. Right around the corner was Smokey Yunick's building and it was on the river, too. I'll bet there must have been 150 Fish Carburetors thrown in there. But I never moved to Daytona. Every time Fireball and them would get started doing something and needed help, they'd run up here and get me.

When I said legends were there, Red Vogt was the preeminent stock car mechanic alive, and Smokey Yunick was right there, too, literally up the road, or river. How big was Red Vogt? He was invited by Bill France, Sr., to the first organizational meeting in the Ebony Room of the Streamline Hotel in Daytona Beach on December 14, 1947. It was then and there Red came up with the name National Association for Stock Car Auto Racing, or NASCAR. If that were not enough, he won NASCAR's first Strictly Stock Car (later Grand National and Whatever Cup) and modified championships. Neil was in amazing company and was tight with Fireball.

Roy Jones owned the first modified car that Fireball ever drove. It was a '40 Ford coupe. Fireball's parents were pretty well off. They owned all the orange groves all the way to Orlando, and Fireball's daddy owned one square city block on the beach with a house in the middle of it. Fireball got his name pitching baseball. He could have had a scholarship to any major college team he wanted to play for. Instead, he left school to drive that old car for Roy Jones. The family got after him and were a little disappointed because they wanted him to play ball.

On the road with a racecar trying to make a living was quite an ordeal, as Neil and Bill Widenhouse, a.k.a. Slab, soon found out. Racing was still a hit-or-miss proposition.

Me and Slab took that '53 Oldsmobile to Miami to run down at Hialeah for Leland. Leland came to Charlotte and got me to go with Slab down there and get it through inspection and whatnot. And we got down there and nobody showed up. They didn't have any cars at all. None. There was me and Slab then Jimmy Lewellen showed up with an old car. They decided they were going to run that race anyway whether they had any cars or not. So they announced to the grandstand that anybody that wanted to race to bring their car on down there and let's go. They brought a new Chevrolet that belonged to the promoter and I got in it. Slab won the race and I finished second. I knew where he was going so I just latched onto him and finished second. I think Jimmy Lew finished third. There's no record of me ever driving that car. I didn't have a NASCAR license. So, therefore, nobody knew you were there. Joe Epton, the chief scorer, knew. The promoter just sent a car down there and I got in it. There wasn't any competition and they let everybody run.

Another day and another track. Then there was another messed-up deal like Hialeah, only different. It was the opposite situation at West Palm Beach.

We had been down in Miami and came back to Fort Lauderdale where they were going to run this half-mile track and everybody that owned a racecar was there. There wasn't any place to get in the racetrack on the pit road. I put a set of tires on that Oldsmobile and put Slab in it and he finished second or third. Then we got down there to West Palm Beach, but they didn't have any people. Nobody showed up in the grandstand. We had cars, but no people. It was getting race time and Johnny Bruner and the promoter were in a big fight. The promoter said he wasn't paying the purse because there was no spectators. Bruner said, "You signed a contract with NASCAR and you're going to pay the purse." Smokey Yunick said, "Look, I'll tell you what. I'm going to take these damn flags and I'm going to start this race. Now y'all decide who the Hell's paying who 'cause we're going to run this race!" They got the cars on the racetrack lined up to run the race, and about the time they were getting ready to start, the lights went out. The promoter took a chain saw out there and cut the power pole down and turned the lights out.

These were the primitive days of organized stock car racing. At Hialeah there were fans in the stands and not enough cars. Then at West Palm Beach, they had all the cars they could ever want, but no fans. At NASCAR's direction

Two. Behind the Wheel and on the Gas

and extremely short notice, Neil and the teams loaded up and headed west of the Mississippi River.

They had a meeting. Johnny Bruner said, "Well, these cars have got to go to West Memphis, Arkansas, and there ain't no time to waste. It's a mile and a half high-banked dirt track and you're going to West Memphis. Take it for what it's worth." Bruner turned to me and said, "Do you have money?" "Well, we got paid first place money down there in Miami." I said, "Slabs got the money. I'll give him a pint of liquor and he won't know where the money went anyway."

We took off and went to Daytona and met on the front porch over there at NASCAR at daylight the next morning. Bruner and Bill France said, "You take your car and go to West Memphis right now. Don't beat around the bush, just go." I talked to Leland and he said, "I'm going to bring the modified. I'll hook it to the pickup and I'll see you in West Memphis." So I met Leland in West Memphis at the Town Park Motel.

When we got there, Buddy had his modified there, but Buddy had wrecked that other modified in Concord, North Carolina, and broke his shoulder. When he broke his shoulder, Shuman quit driving and took over as a NASCAR inspector. He wasn't able to drive with a broken shoulder.

Well, they almost didn't have enough cars to run the Saturday race, but they had enough to run the Grand National race on Sunday. Leland brought an engine with him in the back of the truck from Camden and we put a new engine in that flathead under a tree at the Town Park Motel and went on out to the racetrack. So Leland told me, "Take that old Oldsmobile and start this race and run where you can." This was the first high-banked dirt track.

One problem was I didn't have a helmet with me. Joe Eubanks from Spartanburg brought me a helmet over there and said, "I've got three of them, so you just keep this one." That helmet I ran that first race with in West Memphis is laying downstairs next to the one Fireball gave me.

With a competitor's gift of a lid, Neil Castles raced Leland Colvin's Oldsmobile in the inaugural race at the monster dirt track in Arkansas.

I don't know where I started, but I finished tenth in that race with that Grand National car. That was a big thing towards me getting a ride in a good car. Old man Lee Petty was there with a damn new Dodge, and back then we had a funnel that would hold two milk cans full of fuel. You'd put that funnel in the side of the car and put two milk cans full of fuel in it. He was pitting right above us and that racecar backfired, and that funnel tilted, and set the whole damn pits on fire. He took off out of the pits with that funnel of gas blowing as far as you could see. Some of his pit crew got burned bad that day. That's stuck in my mind.

It is a well-known fact that in the early days of NASCAR, race drivers who drove in races, for one reason or another, often did not get credit for it. Neil mentioned that earlier, saying Chief Scorer Joe Epton knew. This could be for a variety of reasons. In Neil Castles' case, it is likely that on more than one occasion it was because he did not have a NASCAR license. Racing-reference.info reveals that on Sunday, October 10, 1954, at Memphis-Arkansas Speedway in LeHi, Arkansas, the Mid-South 250 was held. There is no mention of Neil Castles competing in that race nor a car owned by Leland Colvin. However, there are comments concerning that race stating Lee Petty was involved in a pit fire and one of his pit crew members was burned. There is no doubt that this is another instance of a driver not being properly credited with competing in a race.

Joe Epton was the Chief Scorer for NASCAR and there was a bunch of modified people that didn't like the way the modified race ended on Saturday. Well, over at the Town Park Motel they got in a fight out there at the swimming pool. Epton had a broken leg and was on crutches. One them old boys with the modified cars picked Joe up and threw him in the damn swimming pool. He couldn't swim. Me and somebody else drug him out of the swimming pool, got his crutches, and took him to his room. Joe Epton was a good friend. Jean and Joe were great friends.

In the midst of all the working and traveling and racing, Neil Castles met his match and her name was Jean.

I had a '55 Ford convertible racecar at that time. I still had those old cars out at Herman's when Waco had those midgets and met Jean. Her sister was head of the NCNB Bank here in town. It's Bank of America now. Well, Jean came down to stay with her sister and we got to dating. I'd go to the race wherever the hell I was going and during the week we'd go out to eat. We got closer and closer and after a year or so we got married. We got married at Wilmore Church. We got a house and when I left to go race, she left with me.

Two. Behind the Wheel and on the Gas

NASCAR's original Chief Scorer Joe Epton with his 1950s-era car battery-powered timing equipment on the Measured Mile at Daytona Beach, Florida (Neil Castles Family Collection).

We hadn't been married long and I bought a '50 Cadillac Coupe de Ville. I was towing that '55 Ford up number one and we were going to Syracuse, New York. I was going through the mountains about three o'clock in the morning and blew the right rear tire off that damn car. Jean was in the back seat sleeping and it about scared her to death. I got out and changed the tire and got on up the road and we stopped to eat. She said, "Don't stop to feed me anything. I don't want to see any food." That tire blowing out scared her to death. Jean went everywhere I went. She was a great companion.

About this time when I had those '55 Fords, they went to '56s, and from there I got tied up with Buck Baker. Me and Buck got along pretty good, too.

Neil "Soapy" Castles

An exciting opportunity to travel overseas and race presented itself to Neil, and he was off with a small group of Americans and their racecars. It was a once-in-a-lifetime opportunity. Truth be told, once in a lifetime would be more than enough. Neil Castles tells it as he lived it.

Greenwood, South Carolina, had a racetrack, a dirt track. The promoter was Buddy Davenport. Buddy Davenport and Lester Vanadore were kind of buddy-buddy with two or three other dirt tracks. Well, they started running cars in England right after the war, but there were not enough cars available. The only cars that were left that wasn't bombed out in England after the Second World War was a joke because I was there.

So in 1955 Buddy Davenport and Lester Vanadore got up with this Digger Pugh in London. Digger Pugh trained all the trapeze acts for Ringling Brothers and Barnum and Bailey Circus. He's got all that trapeze stuff behind his house in London. I had dinner there when he was training those people. He was trying to head up everything with the racecars. Those three decided that they would bring a certain amount of American cars to England for a certain price, a percentage of the gate, and pay for each driver of each car. They were going to hold the World Championship Stock Car Races. Then they made a plan and came back over here and made the deal with Buddy Shuman and with Leland Colvin to send cars to England and they would get this money back. And when we got through racing, whatever was left would be put on a ship and sent back.

I was invited to go and took a '34 Ford coupe of Shuman's to run the first American race in England. It was me, Possum Jones, Crawfish Crider, Bobby Myers, Pete Folse, Bobby Schuyler, and Bill Irick on the *Queen Mary* making that Atlantic crossing.

The British government had safeguards in place so everything would be on the up and up. They were in place, but would they work?

When we got to England, we had to appoint a governor. The British government would not allow the promoters to pay anybody. You had to have a governor that took charge of all the money so the British government would see that there was no money going in and out of the country that they weren't in charge of. So we appointed Lester Vanadore to be the governor and handle everybody's money.

We were going to race at Harringay Arena in London. Billy Graham had a big crusade there and drew I don't know how many hundred thousand peo-

Two. Behind the Wheel and on the Gas

ple. We went in there the next night after Billy Graham finished up and had a race that drew about as many people as he did. All of us was to get a percentage of the grandstand. You're talking thousands of people a night, which was adding up. Ching-a-ling.

They had started their own circuit over there just like NASCAR over here. You had to race with them and the only people that had cars were doctors and lawyers. They would take stuff that the government had discarded and called them racecars. They were racing them at Harringay Arena every week. They wanted these American cars to come in there and run with them. But it wasn't a race, it was a demolition derby. You didn't know who hit who or whatever.

A couple of the traveling racers got a sense that maybe things were not as they appeared and made alternate plans separate from the others. The deal started coming apart.

Crawfish went over to Digger's house and sold him his racecar. He hadn't been there but a few weeks. Bobby Myers sold the car he had over there. They caught the ship and came home before we knew they were gone. They said

Harringay Arena in London, England, when Neil arrived for the World Championship Stock Car Races in 1955. Billy Graham was the previous event (Neil Castles Family Collection).

they had seen that the money was going bad, everything was going bad, and they didn't want to get stranded there. They knew they could sell those two cars and have some money left over. Crawfish Crider and Bobby Myers stayed probably three weeks. They didn't stay and they were gone.

It did not take long before Neil and the other racers also smelled that something was fishy, and it was not England's famous fish and chips.

Well, we had some bad weather and things weren't going too good and we weren't going to the racetrack all that much. We'd go down to this old shop and see about our cars and go on back to the hotel. Me and Possum Jones and Pete Folse got suspicious. The thing wasn't happening. We started asking, "Where's Lester? Lester ain't been around." We took all those racecars and a brand-new Buick convertible over there and that Buick kind of disappeared. Then Lester was gone. So we cornered Buddy Davenport and wanted to know what was going on. Buddy said he had to go to Scotland Yard down there to the police and get the money that Lester was supposed to be in charge

Young Soapy Castles' ride for the World Championship Stock Car Races in 1955. Londoners had never seen anything like this and packed the arena and other venues nightly (Neil Castles Family Collection).

of. Anyway, he went down there for a day and half and came back and he had a passport for every one of us to catch the *Queen Elizabeth* home out of Southampton. We all went there and caught the ship home.

After a month or so, Neil Castles and the remainder of the gypsy racers had headed east to the friendly shores of the United States.

When we got through racing, I came back home on the *Queen Elizabeth* and got off the ship in New York. Bobby Myers and Crawfish had done took off weeks earlier and the rest of us come home on another ship. I caught that Silver Express out of New York to Charlotte that night. I got off at the train station about daylight, caught me a cab, and went down to Shuman's. I had brought back the paperwork from England where we were doing this and

Traveling home in style aboard the *Queen Elizabeth* is Neil, left, an attractive female passenger, and Possum Jones, right. Just off camera to the far right is Pete Folse (Neil Castles Family Collection).

Neil "Soapy" Castles

doing that. They swapped cars around and nobody knew who drove whose car or nothing. Willie was there and I set my suitcase and stuff in the building and went to the house to see Mother.

Buddy Shuman was trying to get stuff straightened out where Buddy Davenport and them took those cars we raced in England and sold them. In the meantime, Ford Motor Company had hired Shuman to build the Schwam Purple Fords. When I got home from England, Buddy said, "Get your butt over here." He told me, "I want you to come over to the hotel in Hickory." I told him I was going to see Jean. "You need to go to work on these Fords." So I went over there and went to work on them Schwam Purple Fords.

Being nobody's fool, Buddy Shuman was far enough removed from the English fiasco that he saw exactly what was going on. He sprang into action and things started popping.

Shuman immediately hired a group of lawyers to get the money that Lester Vanadore had left England with and nobody knew where it was. We run it down to find out that he had come back a week early on the *Queen Elizabeth*. He went to Nashville, Tennessee, and bought out an insurance company with the money he had brought with him. Shuman had the whole bunch indicted and they were after that insurance company in Nashville, and I know there was a lot of enforcement going on about the money. None of us ever saw a dime of our damn money. Now I did get paid $100 a week and all expenses. But the lawsuit was going on big time and it was getting ready to be heard by some judges in a day or two. That was to happen right after the race at Hickory. It appeared that Buddy Davenport and Lester Vanadore took all those cars and the money that came from England, but I don't know that. Nobody will ever know. That was nearly 65 years ago.

Buddy Shuman was going wide-open on multiple fronts and had important missions for Neil to accomplish. Neil acted with equal dispatch.

We had to get the racecars to Hickory, so I went with Willie and the two Schwam Purple Fords for Joe Weatherly and Curtis Turner to run up there. Buddy was already there and was in charge of paying all the hired help and everything through Ford. He said, "I want you to take these reports I'm going to have filled out and carry them with you back to Charlotte and see if Jean or somebody will stick them in the mail in the morning."

Two. Behind the Wheel and on the Gas

Well, I went to the hotel in Hickory that Saturday and Shuman had the reports filled out, everybody's payroll, and put it in a big envelope, and gave it to me to take to Charlotte. He said, "I want you to go to the drug store below the shop on the corner in the morning and meet Frank." Frank was Buddy's brother, Frank Shuman. He said, "I'll have Frank come by and pick you up on that corner 'cause I need you back here for the race and to get the rest of this stuff to Schwam Motors. I want you to be on that corner at 6:30 Sunday morning. Frank will be there waiting on you." So Buddy gave me the paperwork and it was probably 10:30 or 11 o'clock Saturday night. From the time I left there, I came to Charlotte and dropped that stuff off to be mailed.

I went up there to that corner on Sunday morning to meet Frank. I was there at 6 o'clock. Frank drove up and I jumped in the car and said, "We're going to be late." He said, "No, we're not going." "What do you mean we're not going?" He said, "You don't know, do you?" "No." "Buddy got killed last night." I said, "How in the hell did that happen? I just talked to him before I left up there." Frank said, "Well, I don't know what happened either. It's awful fuzzy." Anyhow, they claimed that Buddy got up in the middle of the night to go to the bathroom in that hotel room, run into the door, and hit his head. But that doesn't make sense. Somehow or another he got hit in the head and that room caught on fire. By the time the fire department got there and got Buddy out in the hall, they didn't have any oxygen and he died of smoke inhalation. That's how he died in that hotel room outside the door where they got him out. He wasn't smoking in bed. They had to make up whatever.

The racing world was stunned on November 14, 1955, to read that the great Buddy Shuman had died in a Hickory, North Carolina, hotel fire the day before. Sixty-four years later, Neil is still wrestling with what happened and what could have happened in that hotel room and why.

All that happened was Shuman got hit in the head and was found laying in a hotel room on fire. So I think if the truth ever comes out, and it never will, that the money Lester Vanadore left England with is what got Buddy Shuman killed. I can't say that for sure. I have no proof at all, but that's what I believe happened. All they claimed was Buddy went to sleep with a cigarette in his hand and woke up with the bed on fire, run into the door, and busted his head open. I don't think so because it was probably 10:30 or 11 o'clock when I left there the night before and he was sitting at that desk filling out paperwork. Sometime within about an hour after I left there he was dead.

Neil "Soapy" Castles

He run into the door and killed himself going to the bathroom. Yeah, right. He left a cigarette on the table and caught the bed on fire. That's just a little bit too shady for an old country boy like me to believe. Nobody knows where that money went. And all that paperwork that I collected from Shuman while I was over there, I don't know where it went either. The lawyers that he was dealing with and all that mess just [Neil claps his hands as if to say "vanished"]. When I went to Buddy Shuman's funeral, Lester Vanadore drove up in a brand new white Cadillac convertible.

For the record, the first race of the 1956 season was contested on November 13, 1955, at Hickory Speedway in Hickory, North Carolina. The new 1956 Schwam Purple Fords hit the dirt as Buddy planned. The best showing was by Curtis Turner, who time-trialed third fastest and finished second, right on Tim Flock's Kiekhaefer Chrysler 300's bumper. Joe Weatherly didn't fare quite as well as he gridded seventh and had radiator woes for dismal 28th. But it was dismal anyway and a one-two sweep would not have made any difference.

Neil Castles does not know what happened, but has had 64 years to think about it. The fact is that Neil's opinion, and that's all it is, has not changed over the six decades plus since Buddy Shuman died early Sunday morning on November 13, 1955. Shuman was Neil Castles' father figure, mentor, boss, and most of all, his best friend. For goodness sakes, he nicknamed Neil "Soapy"! But all the soap in the world cannot wash clean the memories of what happened in that smoky Hickory hotel room.

Three

After Buddy

Just after his 21st birthday, Neil Castles' mentor and father figure was gone. Buddy Shuman had conferred upon the youthful Neil the moniker "Soapy," and it was likely used to address him as often as not from then on. Buddy Shuman raced in countless modified races, winning with great regularity. He also ran the NASCAR Speedway Series and Grand Nationals from 1951 through 1955. His lone victory came on July 1, 1952, at Stamford Park, Niagara Falls, Ontario, Canada, the only top-tier NASCAR race ever held north of the border. In his 29 starts on the premier stock car circuit, Buddy claimed one win, four top fives and 16 top tens with points finishes of sixth in 1951 and tenth in 1952. To honor his fabulous achievements in the sport, in 1957 NASCAR created the Buddy Shuman Award, presented each year at the annual award ceremony to individuals and organizations that influenced the growth and development of stock car racing. As of this writing in May of 2018, it has been awarded for 61 consecutive years.

By the 1956 racing season, Neil "Soapy" Castles was on his way, but not yet on his own. He was still building the Schwam Purple Fords that Buddy Shuman got him started on, only now he had a new boss. The big-time driving started on the NASCAR Convertible Circuit with a used car he bought off another driver. Then on March 17, 1957, in Greensboro, North Carolina, he piloted that 1956 Ford number 55 to a 14th-place finish.

Neil officially opened up his lengthy Grand National career on June 20, 1957, in Columbia, South Carolina, in Bill Champion's '56 Ford number 5 for an 18th place. But his next Grand National start was in the biggest race of the year in Bob Colvin's Southern 500 at Darlington. An unexpected phone call got Neil on the big stage.

We were working on building those Schwam Purple Fords for Joe Weatherly and Curtis Turner. Schwam Motor Company was downtown in Charlotte. We also had Schwam Purple Ford convertibles, too. I was right in the middle

Neil "Soapy" Castles

Filthy after a race at Langhorne, Pennsylvania, about 1955 are Neil at left, Don Gray, and Shep Langdon at right (Neil Castles Family Collection).

of that because when I came back from overseas, Shuman had the Ford Motor Company deal. I was still working on them when Turner won the Southern 500 in 1956. I was just there. I wasn't on the pit crew or anything. Buddy had told me that when the [1955] season was over, "I'm going to give you one of those convertibles, the best one, and you can start next year." Pete De Paolo took over the Fords when Buddy died and an old man had the building that Ford took over on Wilkinson Boulevard. I worked there at De Paolo Engineering and that Christmas we bought Pete a big lounge chair and set it under the Christmas tree in his race shop. When he came in for Christmas, we loaded that chair up and shipped it to California. He'd fly in and tell Willie and them in the shop what he wanted to hook up and that's when we started with the overhead Ford engines. Pete De Paolo was very knowledgeable. He knew a whole lot more about what was going on than we did. Pete and Bill Stroppe out in California were very close. That's the reason Stroppe had the Mercury deal. This is where John Holman came into play. John Holman was a good friend of Stroppe, and Stroppe sent him here to take over the Fords

Three. After Buddy

when De Paolo left because he needed somebody on the inside that knew what was going on.

Pete De Paolo was one of the most versatile men in all of auto racing. A fearless driver in the days of no seat belts and cloth helmets, Pete won the 1925 Indianapolis 500 at the first average speed of more than 100 miles an hour. He retired after some serious sheet time in 1934 and became a team owner, winning the 500 in 1935 with Kelly Petillo. As the head of Ford's factory stock car operation for 1956 and 1957 with Neil on the crew, his teams won 21 times in 178 races. When he left there, he was a very popular and hilarious after-dinner speaker and said his greatest thrill was singing "Back Home Again in Indiana" before the start of the 1971 Indianapolis 500. Pete left us on November 26, 1980.

After years of dingy, dimly lit racetracks from West Memphis to London, Neil finally gets the call.

Darlington was a big track and I was glad to get a chance at it. I had been around Darlington with Bob and Leland Colvin all this time and was very familiar with the racetrack. I was there in 1951 with Buddy and a brand-new '51 Ford. Fireball had helped Leland put that sprint car together and Speedy Thompson led the whole race there in 1952 with it until the drive shaft broke on the damn thing on the last lap. So I was very familiar with the racetrack. There was a guy living in Fayetteville, North Carolina, that had two racecars and his name was Spook Crawford. Johnny Allen drove one of Spook's cars.

Well, it was time to go to Darlington and I hadn't come up with a car that I wanted to get involved with. I was trying to buy a new car and couldn't come up with the money. Spook called me and said, "Would you consider driving my second car at Darlington?" "I probably would." "Well, come down here and let's see what we can do with it."

So Jean and I got up the next morning and went down to Fayetteville and over to Spook's. We looked at the old car and seen that we had to move the seat and the seat belts and stuff and did all that. We changed some things around and I agreed to drive that car at Darlington in the 1957 Southern 500. Jean and I spent the night at Spook's, got up the next morning, and I helped Spook load that mess up. Then we took off for Darlington. I started the race in Spook's car. This was car number 68, which was Spook's backup car for Johnny Allen's car number 64.

Neil "Soapy" Castles

Wearing the repaired Fireball Roberts helmet, Neil Castles looks absolutely eager to climb aboard and run what appears to be a Grand National race circa 1957 (Neil Castles Family Collection).

Neil Castles started the eighth annual Southern 500 on September 3, 1957, in 40th place and engine problems had him well behind when tragedy visited again. This time Neil was a witness.

I was on the backstretch and I had a front-row seat to that deal. I had gone to the other side of the tunnel and stopped. I was very close to it, right in the middle of it. Everybody was pitting on the front straightaway and backstretch. Bobby Myers was driving that Oldsmobile of Lee Petty's that had aluminum roll bars in it. It was some kind of deal with NASCAR. There was a lot of beating and banging going on anyway. When Myers' car crashed into Fonty Flock's stopped car, the engine came out of it and rolled down the racetrack. Bobby was killed. He and his brother Billy were good friends of mine, but they never could get along. They always had a fight about something. Bobby went over to Billy's and picked up a cam he'd just had ground and threw it in the floor [and] broke it. That caused a big fight. Bobby didn't run a lot of Grand National racing. He was lucky to get that ride in Petty's car. Billy had the Mercury deal with Stroppe for the hardtops and convertibles.

Myers was killed when he rammed Flock's stalled car on the backstretch. Flock, the 1952 Southern 500 winner, was many laps behind, driving an ill-handling Pontiac owned by three-time Southern 500 winner and two-time champion Herb Thomas. Bobby Myers was driving hard to hold off Paul Goldsmith for the lead when they piled into Flock's car. Neil finished 49th that Labor Day and would be back. He had traveled to England with Bobby Myers and knew him very well. It is not easy for Neil to discuss the crash even though it is over 60 years later. Ironically, Billy Myers would also die in a racecar seven months later, not in a crash, but of a heart attack during a modified race at Bowman Gray Stadium in Winston-Salem, North Carolina, his hometown.

Neil Castles had previously taken on another killer track at Langhorne, Pennsylvania. Built as an oil-based dirt circle in 1926, it had already claimed 13 brave drivers in both AAA and NASCAR events. The area a few hundred yards past the starting line is appropriately called "Puke Hollow." Neil first visited there on May 5, 1957, in his old convertible when he started to the left of Lee Petty in 15th place and retired in 11th position after crashing into Ken Rush. It was a great finish, considering the venue and the outcome.

Langhorne was a mile dirt track circle and I liked it. It was built for sprint cars. You just lined up and kept drifting in the same direction all the time. Being used to the old midgets, I was used to backing into the corner anyway. It fell right in my lap and I loved it. So when you start off, you just cross it up and keep it that way. In that convertible race, two or three cars crashed coming off what would have been the fourth corner right in the middle of that sweep. I slid into them and had to go change the right side tires and all. I don't think we even finished. We just give it up. It was at the end of the race and everybody was beating and banging trying to get another spot.

Thirteen days after his first Southern 500 and in his second Grand National race, he was running with a full field of 48 top-tier drivers in the hardtops back at Langhorne. He started 17th, tucked in behind Emanuel Zervakis, inside of Marvin Panch, and just ahead of Darel Dieringer.

The car ran great all day and I had no problem with it whatsoever. When we got down towards the end of the race, the damn straps on the gas tank broke and it went sailing across the racetrack. The racetrack was real rough and the bolts pulled through the straps that held the gas tank up and it went shooting across the racetrack. I saw it in the rear view mirror when it left. But that was my kind of track and I loved it. I could have stayed there forever.

If you loved Langhorne as he did, then no track was too tough for Neil Castles. The record shows that Gwyn Staley won that 300-miler on September 13, 1957. Neil ran 203 of the 300 laps before the gas tank fell off and he still finished ahead of Speedy Thompson, Tiny Lund, Paul Goldsmith, Marvin Panch, Glen Wood, Jack Smith, Jim Paschal, and 14 others. He risked it all to bring home $125.
About this time Neil got a gift and a number.

There was a car that Ford sent for Tim Flock to drive. I took it to Columbia and Tim run it in the race on that dirt track. When he got out of it he went to that Bill Stroppe Mercury deal and they told me to keep the car and do what I wanted to with it. I painted it and run that car several races. So I went to number 86 because Shuman had already bought the 87 number for him and Baker. In the meantime, Buck decided he wanted Buddy to learn to drive. So I had to go to NASCAR and loan Buddy 86 to run a few races. Then I kept number 86 on my convertible for a long time.

Neil reminisces about a character he had known over the years named Roy Tyner aka "The Wild Indian." Neil and Roy have quite a history.

Roy Tyner was a Pembroke Indian. His daddy was an invalid in a wheelchair and owned a general store in Red Springs, North Carolina. It was the main store downtown and was a general store, a service station, and a garage. Everything in that town belonged to his daddy. He owned the oil company there and had a tractor trailer tanker that Roy drove from Charleston to there once a week with a load of gas and once a week with a load of diesel. Me and Roy were good friends. We traveled on the road together along with everybody else.

In Asheville-Weaverville, I got crashed in that '56 Ford convertible early in the race. Fireball caught me in the quarter panel and I spun and hit the inside guard rail right at the end of the front straightaway. They took me to the hospital in Asheville because I had some broke ribs. About one o'clock

Three. After Buddy

in the morning Roy showed up and said, "I got your clothes. Do you think you'd like to get out of here?" "I'd like to." Him and that cousin of his got me up out of the bed, I got dressed, and we eased on out of the emergency exit of that hospital. Roy had his cousin driving my truck hauling my car. Roy had a new Cadillac convertible. At that time Roy's family was very rich. Well, Roy propped me up in the back of that Cadillac convertible and brought me home to Charlotte.

I got home and Jean was gone to Georgia to visit her brother, who was back from the Air Force. There wasn't anybody there but me and Roy and his cousin Vern, and they sat me down in a big chair in the living room. I managed to get along from there with these ribs until I could get on my feet. I'd get in the kitchen and fix me something to eat.

Anyhow, I went and got that Ford fixed at the shop. It wasn't hurt that bad. I just crunched some sheet metal on the driver's side where I hit the door bar. We just had one door bar and it caught my ribs and broke them. I wasn't that hurt and it wasn't any big deal, but I couldn't do nothing. And that car was number 55 that I bought from Mel Larson. I didn't paint it, I just run up there and started it in the race.

Roy Tyner wanted to go racing like Neil and had the money to get started.

Roy had a pretty nice shop down there and wanted to go big-time racing, but his daddy wasn't doing too well. Roy went up to Lee Petty's brother Julian Petty, who owned the '57 Chevrolets that Bob Welborn was driving. He bought everything Bob Welborn had, hardtops and convertibles, and it all wound up in Red Springs. I don't know what number was on all those damn cars, but I drove one of those '57 Chevrolets a couple of times. Then Julian Petty got tied up with Roy's mother and they left town, went to Florida, and bought a Cadillac dealership. At the end of his racing, Bill France and them got Roy a little help through Pontiac. Nobody had Pontiacs, nobody was fooling with them. Joe Weatherly was the last who had run Pontiacs with Bud Moore. I think NASCAR helped Roy with the Pepsi sponsorship on the Pontiac some, too.

Roy Tyner was a regular in the Grand National and Convertible Divisions from 1957 to 1970, almost the same years as most of Neil's career. Tyner never won in 341 races, but he and his cars number 9 were independent racing fixtures, usually emblazoned with an Indian head and the words "The Wild Indian." It probably was no coincidence that most of his later races were in Pontiacs, once known in racing as "Iron Indians." Unfortunately, on February 23, 1989, Roy Tyner's charred body was found in a burned truck in Conover, North Carolina. He apparently died of a self-inflicted gunshot wound to the head outside of where he worked as show car manager. The truck was used to haul Budweiser and Anheuser-Busch show cars.

Another of the all-time great characters in stock car racing's early days was a transplant from the North who pretty much received a cold shoulder when he first got down South. Fortunately, Neil Castles had known of him for a while.

Tom Pistone come here and had nothing. He had met me at Soldier Field in Chicago in 1953. I was up there with that '53 Oldsmobile of Leland Colvin's. We were starting a race and Norris Friel came over and said, "This one Chevrolet has got the hood welded shut on it. It's going to run. It'll fly. No matter where he finishes in the race, it don't make a damn what he does, you don't see him. He ain't here. No matter if he wins the race, he ain't going to get paid for it. He's going to be hard to deal with." That was Pistone. You see, back then, the Pistones owned Chicago. As far as the Mafia went, they had a bulletproof car for his daddy to come to Daytona to watch the race. That's where the Rupert Seat Belt Company come from. That was one of Pistone's early sponsors and was connected through Chicago.

Sure enough, by 1959 "Tiger" Tom Pistone was sponsored for the season by Rupert Safety Belts and won two Grand National races in a yellow T-Bird number 59 wrenched by fellow Chicagoan Mario Rossi. But way before that, Tom showed up one day at Neil's in a jam.

So he come down here and was hunting him a garage. I was living over at my mother's house with Jean. He come over there and sat down on the porch and said, "Neil, I need help." "What do you need?" He said, "My wife's on the way from Chicago with two truckloads of furniture following her and I'm supposed to have a place for us to stay and I don't even know where to look." I said, "Well, when are you supposed to have this?" He said, "Today." I told Jean, "Get the damn paper and phone book." We started calling this one and another one and found an empty house that could be rented on Barringer Drive in Charlotte. So me and Jean threw him in the car and went to Barringer Drive and looked at that house. We got the people that owned it and rented that house that day. Tom's wife and them got here at midnight that night and started moving in. He lived there about two or three years.

In nearly every instance it appears that Neil Castles helped anybody or any groups of people in dire straits. He and Tiger Tom did not always get along, however, showing that Neil's patience was not limitless.

Pistone and I had our ups and downs. Pistone had a trailer just like the one I had bought from Marvin Panch when he moved here from California. He come over there and borrowed a hub, wheel, tire, and everything off that trailer because he had burnt one up on his trailer. He just wanted to borrow one of mine to put on. I jacked up my trailer out in the yard and took the hub and everything off of it and give them to him. Well, about a year went by and he's still riding on my hub and my trailer is still sitting in the yard on jack stands.

Well, we were in Atlanta at the race and I told the old man that worked with me, "Step get a jack and a couple of wrenches. We're going to get us a hub." We just went down there where all the trailers were and jacked it up, set it on a cement block, took the hub, and walked off. We brought it up there and threw it in the back of the truck.

All at once they realized they couldn't take their car home 'cause they didn't have no hub on the trailer. So here come Pistone down pit road as we were loading our stuff. "Did you get that hub off my trailer?" "Yeah. You've use it long enough. It's time for me to use it." He said, "You can't take that hub." He come back about ten minutes later with the police and told them I stole the hub off his trailer. I told the police that the only reason I stole it was because it belonged to me. The police said, "I believe y'all better work this out."

In 1958, Neil Castles tripled his involvement in the Grand National Division, but backed off with the ragtops. His finishes were unspectacular with a premier league result of 15th in Columbia, South Carolina. He upgraded his '55 Ford to a 1956 model number 86 on both circuits and on the convertible tour saw 19 starts with a best finish of sixth in Richmond, Virginia. He started the season opener on Saturday, February 22, 1958, at the Beach and Road Course on Daytona Beach, Florida.

I've got a letter to me from the State of Florida and the Governor. Great big thing. They sent me a certificate when I run the flying mile on the beach

Neil "Soapy" Castles

at Daytona. The certificate said how fast I run and looked like the title to a car. Tim Flock had the Stroppe Mercury deal and when they started the race that sand just built up in the radiator and it started running hot and boiled all the water out. I made two or three pit stops and I come out of the pits and followed Tim because you couldn't see nothing through those old windshields. So I followed Tim down the beach side and run out on the edge of the water enough to wash the radiator out. Then I lost him. I couldn't see Tim for all that sand. In a few minutes I saw people running every damn where. Tim missed the turn and I followed him right on down the beach. I made a U-turn and went on back and he turned around and come behind me somewhere. We both missed the same turn.

It appears that in that race, Tim Flock was too damaged to continue because he retired due to a crash. However, Neil continued and came home 23rd, falling out nine laps later with gear shift problems.

On Sunday, March 23, 1958, at a convertible race in Richmond, Virginia, Neil again watched as the Grim Reaper pointed his bony finger at one of the real stars and a great driver was gone.

I've sat on this for years. A lot of people know it, but nobody talks about it. When Gwyn Staley wrecked there in the first turn, I was right in the middle of it. All the drivers stopped and jumped out to see if they could help. The car was upside down and they were interested in getting him out without unfastening the seat belt and him fall down and hit the racetrack and break his neck. I was skinny and they held the car up and I slid up under there. I loosened the shoulder harness and let him get loose a little bit while I was holding him up. I asked him, "Am I hurting you? If I start hurting you, you tell me." He said, "I'm not hurting nowhere right now." I asked him, "Do you think you broke anything?" He said, "I don't know." He was pretty well conscious.

Hell, there were ten people with their heads stuck under there hollering, "Neil do this! Neil do that! Neil don't do this! Neil don't do that!" I had more teachers than I'd ever heard of. I was lucky I got anything done. I was doing it the way I felt like I was going to do it or get me out from under there. I started turning him loose and finally got one shoulder loose so he could slide down on me. I got the other shoulder out and he slid down and put his head close to my shoulder and I unhooked the belt and he slid on down.

As he slid down on top of me, the others had my feet and drug me out

Three. After Buddy

from under the car. There was an army of drivers holding that car up and sliding me out from under it. He was laying on me when they drug me out. When I got out, I stood up trying to brush the dirt and mud off me and they were putting him in the ambulance.

That old ambulance took off down the front straightaway and the stretcher rolled out. I don't know exactly how that door flew open or what happened. He died in the wreck, but I'm not sure he died in the wreck. I don't know that when he hit the racetrack it hurt him worse than he got hurt in the wreck. I don't know. I'm not a doctor and I didn't have no idea. But he fell off the stretcher. Hell, there was a thousand people looking right at that. Everybody on the pit road jumped out and started helping get him back on that stretcher and put him back in the ambulance.

You got to remember, I was down in the first corner and this is taking place on the racetrack heading towards the fourth corner. I just saw parts of what was happening and I do know that the door flew open and the stretcher rolled out and hit the racetrack. I don't know what happened to him. He had talked to me earlier and said he didn't think he was hurt that bad. I was afraid I was going to hurt him trying to get him out. Later on they told me he had died after the race. That's what happened that day. I guess his brother Enoch Staley knew all about it. He worked for NASCAR and was the promoter at North Wilkesboro.

Incredible and untold. According to the Spartanburg Herald *of Monday, March 24, 1958, page 1: "Staley was pinned beneath the car as it bounced off the fence. He was dead on arrival at Richmond Memorial Hospital. Doctors said he suffered a fractured skull, several broken ribs, two broken arms, and punctured lungs and heart." That's a lot of injuries for someone that was talking a short time earlier. Neil saddled back up and finished sixth, 13 laps behind winner Joe Weatherly. The record shows that Gwyn Staley started seventh and finished 23rd that day, not making it through the first turn of the first lap, and collected $50. Staley was a top driver in anything he drove. He won three times on the 1957 Grand National tour with wins at Myrtle Beach, South Carolina; Syracuse, New York; and treacherous Langhorne, Pennsylvania. He had captured a fourth in the season opener at Daytona Beach and an eighth a week earlier in North Wilkesboro, North Carolina. He drove for Julian Petty, Lee's brother, and his convertibles for Staley and Champion Bob Welborn were as good as they got.*

Neil has a vivid recollection of an incident at Darlington likely about this time, but it is very elusive to document due to the iffy record-keeping of the day.

There was a car at Darlington that belonged to Bub Strickler. He bought the car from me and couldn't get along with it at all. He asked me would I qualify it and start it in the race and then let him have it. I said, "Well, I don't know about that. I'll qualify it, but I want to run the whole race." I started that car and ran it up until a matter of a few laps to go and I had to make a gas stop. He jerked the damn seat belt off and said he was driving the rest of the race. So I got out and he put his butt in it. He made two laps and went down in the middle of one and two and rolled it end over end. He came walking back up through there and I said, "You fixed that one, you got another one?"

Undoubtedly, one of the oddest tracks they ran on back in those days was a little quarter-mile track in Asheville, North Carolina, named McCormick Field. It was laid out around the perimeter of the baseball field where the Asheville Tourists still play. Neil Castles recalls it well.

I run on that little quarter-mile track in Asheville that went around the ball park, McCormick Field. I had run midgets on it and I hated it because you'd go down to home plate and take a left and slide on around. They widened it to run sportsman races there every week. Me and Baker had two cars and I took one up there. It was just tight getting it around there. It was like a bull in a china shop. So I run the whole race right down to the end and coming off the fourth corner, I was leading the race, blowed the engine, crankshaft come through the bottom of the pan, cut the steering linkage in two, the right front wheel caught the wall and I rolled it down the front straightaway. Well, I got the thing loaded up and went back to the shop. Baker called the next morning and said, "Well, I'm glad to see you made the headlines. This morning you're on the front page. How did you engineer that?" I said, "Very carefully." He said, "Is everything all right?" "Yeah, all we need is another car."

A different and unique twist came to Neil Castles' life in the mid-1950s, and as many times in the past, Bob Colvin was the catalyst. In the long run, it was most definitely a life-altering event.

Three. After Buddy

Neil Castles and his trusty 1956 Ford convertible number 86 prior to the inaugural Rebel 300 in Darlington, South Carolina, on May 10, 1958 (Neil Castles Family Collection).

Bob Colvin made a film every year and he had a producer in New York named Les Richter. He came to Darlington once a year and provided all the information needed to make a Darlington film that you could show to promote Darlington Raceway everywhere. At that time, nobody had ever put a camera in a car and he wanted to put a camera in a car. Bob met with Bill France and France said that it was out of the question. "One of those damn old cameras flying off one of the cars and hurt somebody, we'd never get out of the lawsuits. It's not going to happen." I said, "If I mount one beside me on the roll bar, is that going to hurt anything?" He said, "If you put it where nobody can get hit by it and it's mounted solid, you make the mount, and I'll see if I'll approve it." France said he wasn't going to tie up anything on pit road fooling with a picture show. I made a camera mount for one camera on an extra roll bar. I filmed the start of the race. I filmed the first caution flag.

I had about four switches taped to my leg and run the camera without having to stop and fool with it. Well, I got it all done and the Darlington film that year turned out very good. Bob Colvin was happy with it.

Soon Neil was getting offers for movie driving and stunt work, and in 1958 he filmed the Robert Mitchum classic Thunder Road *by D.R.M. Productions and United Artists. According to the Internet Movie Database (IMDb), Neil Castles, Sr., is listed as "stunt driver (uncredited)," "Carey Loftin (stunt coordinator)," and "Dale Van Sickel (stunts)." The movie was shot in the Asheville and Brevard, North Carolina, areas and was released May 10, 1958.*

The stunt coordinator on that show knew that I was doing stunts and called me to come up there and work two or three days. The reasons the producers did not want to give you credit was because they had to put you in the Screen Actors Guild [SAG]. That means you draw residuals off of it every time it's shown. So none of the directors would give you credit for anything you were doing. The whole thing we were doing was bootlegging film and I didn't have enough sense to know any better. Every time I'd do some of this stuff off the wall, they'd keep calling me as long as they didn't have to pay any residuals. That's the bottom line. I did hundreds of things that nobody will ever know I did it because nobody wanted to pay residuals.

Stunt work began literally rolling in, and in 1959 Bob Colvin came up with an idea. Neil performed stunts and had an acting role in the theatrically released stock car racing movie Thunder in Carolina. *Produced and released in July of 1960 by Howco International Pictures, it was directed by Paul Helmick, a veteran assistant director usually associated with Howard Hawks. Some of Helmick's credits, and uncredits, were the highly acclaimed* To Have and Have Not, Gentlemen Prefer Blondes, How to Marry a Millionaire, River of No Return, Marty, Rio Bravo, Hello, Dolly!, *and many others.* Thunder in Carolina *starred big-name actor Rory Calhoun, with later to be Gilligan's Island skipper Alan Hale, Jr., Connie Hines of* Mr. Ed *fame, and a host of local talent. A large part of the film used the 1959 Southern 500 as a backdrop and integral part of the plot. Other important scenes were filmed on the third-mile dirt of Hartsville Speedway in Hartsville, South Carolina. That particular Southern 500 was filled with thrills and spills and others that Hollywood added, performed by one of the great stuntmen of all time, Carey Loftin, and the young racer, Neil Castles. However, Neil is listed in IMDb with the actors as "Neil*

Three. After Buddy

Neil's first screen credit was 1960s *Thunder in Carolina*. Over the opening action on the Hartsville Speedway in South Carolina, Neil is listed before veteran stunt man Carey Loftin (Perry Allen Wood Racing Archives).

Castles Sr., Grand National race driver." The film's opening credits bill him under "Special Stunts" with Carey Loftin.

I had been doing some motion picture work for different people and Bob said, "I'll tell you what. We're going to make a movie and I want you to do it. You get the cars, the people, I'll put together the production, and we're going to make a movie." I got hired to do *Thunder in Carolina* at Darlington. Rory Calhoun, Alan Hale, Jr., Connie Hines, they were there every day we filmed it and I got to know them pretty well.

I bought three '57 Chevrolets and painted them all just alike for the movie. In the first one I hit the guardrail in turn one with it, went through it, turned it over, and tore it up. That was the end of that car. It left. According the story, a racecar has to dodge a wrecked racecar in the middle of the racetrack and there wasn't a wrecked car there. They set up a camera location on top of a scaffolding in one and two. That was where the principle car had to turn right and go through the rail to miss the one in the middle of the track. Where that car was to go through the rail, I flipped another one and blocked the racetrack with it. That was one of those number 9 cars. To wreck this car

Neil "Soapy" Castles

While filming *Thunder in Carolina* in September 1959 at Darlington Raceway, Neil looks back with Rory Calhoun, aka Mitch Cooper, riding shotgun as he pulls Cooper's 1957 Chevrolet onto the track (Neil Castles Family Collection).

in the middle of the racetrack, I had to hit the rail on the right side in turn one. We put a mark on the guardrail and that was my mark. I went into one ever how fast that old Chevrolet would run and hit the rail right there, the right front wheel went up the rail, hung, rolled three or four times down from the top of the guard rail, and landed in the middle of racetrack. I got out of it and walked off. I didn't think anything about it.

Well, that was the beginnings of some of the stunt work that they liked. I don't what I was paid to get it done. The main thing was that Bob Colvin wanted it done and I had been dealing with the Colvins almost all of my life. If Bob said, "Let's do it," then we done it. I got along fine with Rory Calhoun. I did another movie with him later on. But this was just like an everyday job to me. We all stayed at the Darlington Motel. Weatherly and Turner stayed there, too.

Three. After Buddy

Neil Castles hits his mark, rides the guardrail, and rolls the Chevy to land upside down in the middle of Darlington Raceway filming *Thunder in Carolina* in 1959 (Neil Castles Family Collection).

Casually strolling over to the crowd of onlookers, Neil has completed his crash job in turn one at Darlington Raceway filming *Thunder in Carolina* in 1959 (Neil Castles Family Collection).

A particularly dramatic scene is when a blue 1957 Ford number 91 driven by the fictional and very hung-over "old pro Tommy Webb of Kokomo, Indiana," is in the pits prior to his qualifying attempt. In a close-up, Neil stands next to the racecar with a clipboard and says, "When do you want the green flag, Tommy?" Webb, played by stunt man Carey Loftin, weakly holds up two fingers and Neil responds, "In two laps? Hey, Tommy, are you OK?" With that, Loftin lays rubber out the pits, and a lap and a half later flips to his fiery death on the backstretch, not far from where Bobby Myers actually died two years earlier in the Southern 500. In viewing the scene today, notice the skid marks where no doubt a couple of practice crashes were tried.

I bought that car, a blue '57 Ford, in Georgia from a boy that raced Grand Nationals with us. Carey was handling all of the stunts. Carey did that

Neil confers with veteran stunt man Carey Loftin, aka Tommy Webb, before roaring to his movie death in time trials. Note the wire running up Neil's pants to capture his speaking part (Neil Castles Family Collection).

stunt because they wanted me up there talking to him when this was going to happen.

In the official results of the 1959 Southern 500, Neil Castles is listed driving 1957 Ford number 91, running at the finish in 37th place. It is reasonable to believe Neil got credit for the race, no matter who drove the car, since he bought it. It is also likely that he was 272 laps behind winner Jim Reed due to frequent stops for film or whatever else was needed for the movie. The fatal crash scene was probably filmed after the race when the car became expendable. It is not found in the records of any other Grand National race.

He probably did not realize it, but certain people were noticing Neil Castles for more than just his racing. Word of mouth a continent away was going to be life-changing someday. Another movie opportunity came rather quickly.

Cast members of *Thunder in Carolina* are, from left to right, Buck Baker (driver and actor), John Hines (actor), Neil Castles (stunt driver and actor), and Rory Calhoun (actor) (Neil Castles Family Collection).

Neil "Soapy" Castles

I made that movie up there in Hillsborough, *Death of a Race Driver*. Man, it was cold. It had been sleeting all morning and I was about to freeze. The stunt man that was supposed to do the stunts was late and finally didn't show up at all. So they came and asked me to do it since I had helped out with *Thunder in Carolina*. Buck had that old Chevrolet and I used it.

They borrowed a car, one of them old Mercuries, from Fred Harb. Fred agreed to rent it to them as long as they didn't burn up the inside of it. I was supposed to run it off the racetrack up in one and two and turn it over down through there. So they got it all lined up and came over there and put an old uniform on me and I was racing with Lee Petty, as far as the movie goes. I'm supposed to pass Lee on the outside and he's to move up and hit me and I'm to go over the bank and roll the car, which that was no big deal.

Richard Petty came up there and said, "Daddy wants to know how you want him to hit you." I said, "You tell that old man with as many people as he's run over if he can't get this car out of the way he should have stayed at home." But that Chevrolet was one of them damn Speedy Thompson Chevrolets. I bought it. They wanted me to do it with the Mercury instead of the Chevrolet. Anyway, I stayed on the outside and Lee came under me and kept moving up. I moved up until I dropped the right rear wheel off and when it went off the side of that dirt bank, there I went.

End over heels I went, and there was a creek down there and I got in that creek and scooped that thing full of mud because the windshield was done gone. I got between two pine trees and they told me I couldn't get out until they hollered "Cut." I hung there forever. I thought they would never say anything. I reached up there and unhooked that seat belt and fell down in the roof of that cold muddy-ass car. It was really freezing in that water. I crawled out through the windshield, come up the bank, and Fred Harb was up there hollering, "Y'all can't burn my car up." I said, "Go down there and tell them to give you a check."

The stunt Neil had to perform to kill off Buck Larson's antagonist involved a 1957 Ford number 22 that doubled for the car in the actual Hillsborough race footage of Buck Baker battling it out with Fireball Roberts' number 22 1957 Ford.

That car didn't even have an engine in it. So Lee Petty got out there and put his front bumper on my back bumper and shoved me around the track. When we got to the first turn, I eased the car over the bank and flipped several

Three. After Buddy

times. This time I got out and the movie people came over there and doused it with gas and set it on fire. Supposedly the smart-ass driver got killed and I won the race. Well, my truck was parked over there by Speedy Thompson's truck and Speedy had a 55-gallon barrel of full of wood and a good fire going. I jumped up in the back of that truck and took the uniform off and this guy's standing out there hollering, "Give me that uniform. I've got to have it!" Speedy handed me my dry shirts and pants that I had on before I put that uniform on. I threw that guy that wet-ass uniform and said, "You wear it."

It was next that Neil got a straight-from-the-heart endorsement from someone who knew his way around a movie set and was a major name.

I put on my warm jeans and shirt and was getting about half wiped up with some towels Speedy had in the back of the truck and this big limousine drove up right behind us. A guy got out and come around there and said, "The man in the back seat of the car wants to talk to you." "I hope he's got something good to say." The guy said, "He probably has." I got down and went over there and opened the door on that car and got in the back seat. That guy says, "Anybody ever tell you you could get hurt doing that?" I said, "No, but I've had a few times I thought I could anyway. By the time you get changed and collect your money it's time to go home." He said, "Well, I tell you what, if you ever need a job, here's my business card. Give me a call. I can get you a good job and you don't have to be near as dangerous doing it. I liked it, but I don't agree with doing it the way y'all did it. Give me a call." I started to get out of the car and he reached under the seat and handed me a fifth of liquor. "It's kind of cold today. This might warm you up." That fifth of liquor is setting down there in the basement. The big shot in the car was James Whitmore. I was sitting in the back seat of that limo with James Whitmore. He said, "I like to look good, but I don't want anybody getting hurt for me. You could get killed doing that." The stuff I did later on was built from there.

The name of the project was actually Death at the Stock Races *and was a half-hour episode of a CBS anthology series called* Suspense. *IMDb lists it as* I, Buck Larsen, *and it aired on April 15, 1964, although it was filmed around the winter of 1959 at Occoneechee Speedway in Hillsborough, North Carolina. It was written by the prolific Charles Beaumont and directed by the even more prolific Frank McDonald. James Whitmore plays Buck Larsen, who is seen clev-*

erly driving Buck Baker's Black Widow 1957 Chevrolet number 87 in actual Hillsborough footage and that staged involving Neil. Twice Oscar-nominated, Whitmore won a Best Supporting Actor Golden Globe for Battleground in 1950 and an Emmy in 2000 for Outstanding Guest Actor in a Drama Series for The Practice. The rest of the cast included Vic Morrow as the antagonist Tommy Linden, who drives a Fireball Roberts look-alike 1957 Ford number 22, and another actor/driver with a bit part named Joseph Campanella, who is still active as of this writing. With three Hollywood stunt projects under his belt and solid auto racing career, Neil Castles was a sought-after individual on multiple fronts. Neil was doing stunts upon request and it was so frequently and so long ago that he does not even remember for whom he did many of them.

This guy was a big photographer for the *Charlotte Observer* and they wanted a picture of a car going through a billboard in the air. He came over there wanting to know if I could this, that, and the other. We got the billboards up and we figured out how to do it. Well, it worked and they thought that was great. So two weeks later he wanted me to spin a car underneath the boxcar of a moving train. The train engineer said, "How do I even know that I'm going to be able to hit the brakes? How long are you going to be under that boxcar?" I said, "Long enough to get out." He said, "I'm going to watch." "OK. You watch and we'll do it." I got an old car and I tried it. I broke it loose and spun it sideways under that train and got out from under it three times. I don't know what they ever used it for. So

Neil with Erwin George "Cannon Ball" Baker about 1960. Baker was a pioneer motorcycle and automobile racer in the early 1900s and the first commissioner of NASCAR (Neil Castles Family Collection).

anyhow, he was the big photographer for the *Charlotte Observer* for many years.

Years later, Richard Petty was filming a TV thing at Rockingham. The car had to go across the racetrack, spin, and all kinds of stuff. They came up there and asked me if I'd do it. I had done maybe eight or ten spins at Rockingham right down the middle of the front straightway. I don't know who the stunt coordinator was or anything else. There was nothing ever documented that I did it. As far as I know, nobody knows that I did it except me and two or three more. The word of mouth got around, "If you want it done, I know who will do it."

For now, however, there were thousands of miles of stock car racing to go, and all that goes with it. Neil Castles must have had an angel on his shoulder and a horseshoe up his, well, you get the idea. He was young, handsome, and living life at its fullest with loving wife Jean backing him all the way. Soapy was only just getting started.

Four

Racing into the '60s

The 1950s found Neil Castles racing on different teams and fielding his own hardtops and convertibles. He also had more experiences with the dream makers, the folks from Hollywood, that one day would totally replace racing as his livelihood. But before the movies took him over, Neil had a lot of racing to do. As he had found in the past, it was sometimes overwhelmingly bad. There are things that Neil has seen and been involved with that are very hard to remember and even harder to talk about decades later. One of those times relates to the 1960 Southern 500 at Darlington. Again, death visited there along the backstretch as in 1957, only this time in triplicate. Neil saw it and involuntarily got involved. He very reluctantly tells it in a hushed, reverent voice.

    I was in the race in a hot old car that the water was boiling out of it. When the wreck happened I came down the pit road to get water poured in it. Roy Tyner and Bobby Johns banging fenders was what started it. That was when Joe Taylor got killed. He was my Sunday school teacher at Wilmore Presbyterian Church. He was on the outside of the pit wall and when the car hit, it cut his legs off and his body fell over in the racetrack. I don't know how to tell that story. I saw Paul McDuffie damn near as high as the grandstand in the air. Bobby Johns hit him.

    Well, I was sitting there in the car afterwards and Bob Colvin came over and said, "I need you to go with the police and identify who is actually dead." So I unbuckled the seat belt and got out of the car and went with the police to the hospital in Florence. When we got to the hospital they took us down to this room and they called it "The Bleeding Room." All of the bodies had been brought in there and put in the floor in that bleeding room. Bob sent me over to identify McDuffie, a mechanic Charles Sweatlund, and Mr. Taylor. I didn't like that idea at all.

    After I identified them we were coming out of the door of the hospital and we met Mr. Taylor's brother and his son coming in the door. He grabbed me by the arm and said, "Neil, how's everybody?" I said, "I don't know. I couldn't find out." I'd done been in there and identified them being dead. I couldn't talk about that. I just left. The police took me back and I told Bob what I'd seen and he said, "Well, you've seen it, now you've never seen it. Forget it." They took those people in that room to bleed; to bleed out. We poured some water in that old car and I got back on the track with it for a little bit. It had gotten so hot the gaskets were gone, so I just quit.

Unthinkable. This horrible incident took place nearly 60 years ago and Neil Castles does not want to remember it, let alone talk about it; he did not at first, even want to use it in this book. The fact that he left the track, went and identified the dead which he knew well, and came back to get in a rag of someone else's car to re-enter a race in which he was hopelessly behind is beyond imagination. NASCAR records of the race do not record Neil as a participant in the 1960 Southern 500. Memories are a tricky thing, especially very bad ones. There is no doubt that Neil Castles' eyewitness account of the accident and the terrible task thrust upon him by Bob Colvin is 100 percent true. The belief here is that rather than NASCAR's records being so far off, Neil was probably in the race as a relief driver. Few if any records of relief drivers were kept by NASCAR in those days and that explains it satisfactorily.

In 1960 and 1961, a particularly ugly episode in NASCAR history took place and Neil Castles was involved in it, too. Curtis Turner, president of debt-strapped Charlotte Motor Speedway, was trying to pay for construction at the track that was completed in 1960. He had a deal with Jimmy Hoffa and the Teamsters Union that they would bankroll the speedway if Turner could organize a race drivers' union. Tim Flock was with him on the deal. Bill France would have none of it. Originally, many of the drivers, thinking it was about better, safer racing facilities, a pension plan, and other noble pursuits, were all for it and backed Turner and Flock. But as Big Bill's gun-toting opposition proved unshakable, the unionization attempt failed. It cost organizers Curtis Turner a four-year "lifetime" ban and Tim Flock was effectively drummed out for life. Neil had already dealt with Curtis several times over the years.

I went with the bunch. I didn't want Turner to get thrown out. We had gone back and forth on old cars for years. I let Turner drive my car in 1957 at the Peach Bowl in Atlanta in a convertible race one time. I'd already qualified and Ralph Moody was running around like a chicken with his head cut off. Turner was leading in the points and they didn't have a car for him

Neil "Soapy" Castles

because they'd wrecked his coming down the road. He said, "You going to let him start your car in the race?" I answered, "What? What are you going to do for me? You walk on our heads every day and now you need a little help." Well, Turner didn't have a car, and I said, "Curtis, get in this damned old car and start it. Don't tear it up because I don't have another one." He ran a few laps in it and parked it and I got in it and finished the race.

But I didn't care about the union because I wasn't a union person. I never had dealt with a union. I never had to deal with a union until I got in the motion picture business. Then I had to deal with the Teamsters, Screen Actors Guild, and others in the motion picture business. When Turner and them decided to buy that property for the speedway, they didn't do any soil sampling or nothing. The whole north end of that thing was solid rock. On the morning of the first race, they were blowing rock out of the north turn. The dynamite was throwing rocks all the way across the highway out there. They had the highway blocked.

But Turner had come to me and said, "When this thing comes down to the line, who are you with?" I said, "Well, don't look around, but I might be behind you." That was my way of putting it. "I'm not signing nothing to agree to nothing. We'll see how it boils down and if it works out, I might be right behind you."

So Neil refused to commit to the union, mainly because he did not care one way or the other. He wanted to race and that's all. If it meant joining the union to do it, he probably would have. But the unionization failed and Neil Castles continued on unfazed.

Often in Neil Castles' career he went out of his way to help others, almost to a fault. One time in particular he was doing something for his competition and it could have been devastating to his career and life in general.

You see this book you gave me that you wrote on Bud Moore, with you and Greg's autographs in there? Well, we were at Daytona getting ready to qualify years ago. It was me and Cotton and Goldsmith and whoever. We had five Dodges on pit road and actually we were waiting for the sun to go down a little and cool the track some.

We got to talking and being as how it was cooling off in the evening, we could up the timing on them cars about three degrees and that would pick us up a mile an hour on qualifying. As hot as it had been, if we went up three degrees earlier, it would have burned a hole in the piston. I told one of mechanics, Bill Step, "Step, go over there and get my timing light out of the

Four. Racing into the '60s

truck. We're going to up this timing." He come back and we started up at the top end of the line with Goldsmith and come down through there with me and Cotton and at 3,000 RPMs we were bringing the timing up three degrees. You'd loosen the bolt on the distributor and I had the timing light in my right hand and turning the distributor with my left hand just real slow to make sure I didn't go more than three degrees.

Well, there was a thousand people on pit road anyway, and somebody hit my elbow and my hand went in the fan and the timing light went into a million pieces. I pulled my hand back and looked at it and reached back and got a rag I had and just laid my hand in that rag. I wrapped the rag around it and went right behind the pit wall into the infield hospital. I walked in there and said, "Y'all want to take a look at this?" That guy said, "No! Cover it up! We can't do anything for you here. You've got to go to Halifax Hospital immediately. I'd send you, but we don't have but one ambulance and we need it here because we're getting ready to qualify. Have you got a car somewhere?" "Yeah, I got a car parked down there at the scoring stand." He said, "Go get it and go to the emergency room and I'll have them expecting you."

So I walked in over at the emergency room and this nurse wanted to know if she could help me and I told her. She said, "Oh yeah, they called from the racetrack and said you were coming over here. Sit down there a minute and we'll see what we can do." I sat down there in a chair and my hand was leaking pretty good and she went and got a pan and she said, "Let's put a pan under there." This doctor come over there and looked and I uncovered it and some fingers were cut off. He said, "Well, we can stick them back on there, but I don't know how much good it will do." They throwed me on a gurney and took me to the operating room and I was in and out of there for two days. They went up my arm and pulled this stuff back down and tied things together and said, "You won't be able to use it, but it will look better." When they got through with it, my hand was all in a cast, but I made them leave this thumb out so I could hook it on a spoke of a steering wheel and guide it with my left hand.

Meanwhile, somebody else qualified my car and raced it, I don't remember who, because they wouldn't let me out of the hospital 'cause they had those things tied up in my arm. Jean stayed at the motel until they let me out of the hospital. When I got my hand out of the hospital, whoever was with us hooked up the racecar and brought it back to Charlotte. We had a brand-new Ford station wagon and Jean come to the hospital and got me and we come home.

Neil "Soapy" Castles

I'll tell you what a good job they do over there at Halifax Hospital. See where he sewed that back together and didn't even wipe the grease off of it? He left the grease on that finger and just sewed it on in there.

When I got home, my fingers were stiff just like that. You couldn't bend them. I couldn't touch nothing with my fingers. All the nerves were tied in knots. Well, every time in a race I'd run in a corner to make a left turn, this one finger would hit the roll bar and you'd about break the seat belt it hurt so bad. You'd be turning the steering wheel and if you turn it too far that finger would hit that roll bar and I put up with that for a month. I come home when we were living over on Sullins Road and sat down in the kitchen. I told Jean, "This hand's got to go. I've had enough trouble with it." So I interlocked my hands under the table and hit them twice between my knees and I broke every one of those fingers. Jean was sitting there and blood flew everywhere. From being stiff, I broke all of them back. Well, I don't have much feelings in the ends of them at all now, but I can use them. Since then, I go to some of them autograph sessions and scratch off my autograph, but my signing ain't too good. I can take an old grease pen and get by. So I figure if this book goes like we want it to, somebody will want me to sign it. I have been sitting down in my spare time trying to improve my writing with this hand so I can autograph this book.

I hadn't expected Neil to refer to the Bud Moore book, and I never like to refer to myself in these writings. But how could that be left out? At nearly 84 years old, Neil Castles is brushing up on his handwriting decades after his life-changing Daytona pit road mishap in anticipation of autographing this book. He is one incredible man! Pit road is always a dangerous place and caution is the rule, what with all the people, cars, fuel, you name it, that could hurt you. That is why Neil Castles was always all business there. No sir! No clowning around.

We were at Charlotte Speedway and I was driving a '48 Harley Davidson. There's a picture of me and Chuck Stansell on it, us standing on each other. Well, Bob Osiecki with the Dodge deal had a big goat out on pit road, [because] Dodges were called "goats." They said, "Let's have some fun. Put that goat on that motorcycle." So they loaded the goat on the motorcycle and I think I'm the only one that made four laps of Charlotte with a goat on a motorcycle. The only reason it ended when it did was the goat got his foot on that hot exhaust pipe and was having a damn fit. I come down pit road

Four. Racing into the '60s

and dumped him off. That's where you saw me and Chuck and a mechanic that came from Chicago to help Baker on a car, all on that motorcycle. They were wanting to ride up and down the pit road on it, too. They said if somebody else would get on top and make it three that would look good. Hunter was there making pictures. So I jumped up on a box setting on back of a truck, jumped on the back of Chuck, and said, "Let's go!" And that's the picture of the three of us on that '48 Harley of mine.

Apparently for Neil and his pals, caution that day was thrown to the wind. Could one imagine anything close to that happening today?
The Cotton Owens thread comes up a lot in the fabric of Neil Castles' life. It is quite obvious that they had a long and enduring friendship, and not just because they were both Dodge Boys. It was cemented with acts like an undated incident after a race at Darlington.

So we went to run at Darlington. When the race was over, Cotton had wrecked his car all to hell. It was tore all to shit. He come over there and said, "Neil, what would you charge me to haul my car to Spartanburg? I could cut it up in two pieces and haul part of it home and come back and get the other part tomorrow." I said, "That's going to be a lot of work, Cotton, to cut that car up and haul it to Spartanburg in two pieces. And I don't know how I could charge you to haul your car to Spartanburg when I'm hauling my car to Charlotte. If you want a deal on this thing, I'll tell you what you do. I got a tow bar for my car that all I got to do is snap it to it. I don't have to have it on the trailer. You put the tow bar on my car, and you hook it to your truck, and you take it to your shop in Spartanburg. I'm going to load that wrecked car of yours and we'll take it to your shop and unload it and I'll get my car from you and put it on my trailer and go home." So I took that wrecked car to Spartanburg and put it in the shop and loaded my car up and me and Jean went on home.

After that, I needed to buy some old stuff and an old car and all. I went down there to Spartanburg and talked to him and he sold me stuff out of his junkyard. He had a pretty good deal with Chrysler and had a lot of good stuff and I was buying some of it. And he treated me right on it. Me and Cotton kind of become friends on account of me hauling that damn car for him from Darlington. After that he felt like he owed me something, but he didn't owe me nothing.

Clowning on pit road at Charlotte Motor Speedway in May 1962 with, top to bottom, Neil, Chuck Stansell, and Buck Baker's unnamed mechanic from Chicago aboard Neil's 1948 Harley Davidson (Neil Castles Family Collection).

One of the unsung gentlemen of stock car racing was Marvin Panch. He was a Californian who came east to race Fords in the 1950s, won the Daytona 500 in 1961, and was always a front runner. Neil hooked up with him on a deal sometime in the 1960s.

Four. Racing into the '60s

Marvin Panch come to Charlotte and opened a brake shop down on Morehead Street to put brakes on passenger cars 'cause he had a job with Grey Rock. When he come here he had an old racecar and a trailer and a truck. Well, he had that old trailer and wanted to sell it. He needed to get some money out of it so I bought it. That trailer was so ill-handling that if you hooked it to a pickup truck it would go sideways down the highway. I had to put vacuum booster brakes on my truck and hook vacuum booster brakes to the trailer so every time you'd get sideways you'd just hit the brakes and it would straighten you up. I finally got it fixed by changing the axles around and with the vacuum booster brakes it was great. So I was the only one in NASCAR that had a trailer. I put a floor on that trailer out of real thick marine plywood and put dividers in it. I had front end parts on one side and rear end parts on the other side. I put everything that you needed so that you didn't have to have a truck to haul it. On top of it I put a big lid and you'd shut the lid and put two pins in it and all your parts was enclosed in the bottom of that trailer. It added enough weight to that trailer to stop that fishtailing.

Neil is listed with no Grand National starts in 1961 and just eight in 1962. He recalls some wonderful stories of another great driver of that period, Larry Frank.

He come to Charlotte to drive an old car for Ike Kiser. Ike Kiser had a junkyard and a wrecker service over here off North Tryon Street. He had an old dirt track car that they'd been running periodically one place or another. I don't even know who was driving it. Larry Frank went over there and talked Ike into letting him drive that car if he could get it ready to run. Larry didn't have nowhere to live. He was basically trying to get started somewhere. At Ike's shop office, there was a landing up there where they used to store stuff. He stacked up tires all the way to the ceiling all the way around that thing and left one opening. He put him a bed up there and made his living quarters in the top of that garage until he could run the first race.

Larry Frank more than paid his dues and won the 1962 Southern 500, but not before it was originally awarded to Junior Johnson, who got the Victory Lane interviews and kissed the queens. Frank's new light-blue Café Burgundy Ford Galaxie number 66 had an interesting birth. Naturally, Neil Castles was right in the middle of it.

Now, Larry Frank won the Darlington race. He had a brand-new car that had just been built. The car was built in me and Jean's basement. Where we lived, I had a basement that you could park four or five cars in. Larry got that car and brought it over to the house and him and Ralph Moody and a lot more got everything they needed from Holman and Moody and built that car and Larry won the race with it. Bill Shockley was working on that car. They were staying at our house. They were sleeping in the living room, dining room, kitchen on the table, sleeping bags everywhere. Jean cooked enough breakfast every morning for 30 people. Ralph Moody was part of Holman and Moody so he didn't steal the parts. He just didn't let John Holman know he was holding some of them. Larry moved to Greenville, South Carolina, and him and Bill Shockley opened up a Go Kart shop they run together for three years.

And how did Larry Frank spend the 1962 Southern 500 winnings?

Larry bought an airplane after he won Darlington. We got to asking him, "How do you know where you're going?" He said, "I went to the store and got me a new pair of binoculars and I can follow any Interstate you put me on."

It was Larry Frank who one day was able to repay Neil for the friendship and help when moving south from Indianapolis. As always, Neil does not expect repayment.

Later on I had that Chrysler 300 of Buck Baker's hooked to my pickup truck going down 85 in Greenville heading for Atlanta. The old boy that run around with me, Bill Step, was a state highway patrolman. He wanted to ride with me down there and watch the race and come back. We're going right down the outside lane and a truck in front of me dumped off a chunk of steel and I hit it. I slid sideways down in the damn median with the tow bar getting bent and twisted and I'm getting on the gas trying to control it. So here I am sitting in the middle of the damn median grass with everything I got tore up and flat tires. Busted all the tires. I unhooked what we had left of the tow bar and throwed it in the back of the damn truck. Me and Step jumped in that damn truck and went right up there on White Horse Road to where Larry Frank had a Go Kart shop. I throwed the tow bar out there and told Larry to go to welding on it. I told him I had to have some racecar tires and somebody in Greenville had a Grand National car and brought me four wheels and tires and put them on that racecar. Larry welded up the tow bar and we hooked up and went right on to Atlanta.

In 1963 Neil had formed an official alliance with Buck Baker, whom he had known for years. It was a teaming that would last over four years and nearly 200 races. The friendship went much longer.

I ran out of cars. I didn't have a car and me and Buck had been dealing together. Speedy and Buck had '57 Chevrolets in Spartanburg. When that kind of blew up, Speedy came to the house on Wilmore Drive and got me and we went to Spartanburg and brought them '57 Chevrolets to the shop. Then Baker got that Chrysler deal in '61 and '62. Buddy was number 86 and Buck was number 87. The Chryslers started running pretty good. He ran it a lot of races and I ran it a lot of races. That's when the numbers started changing a lot. If Buck didn't like it, he'd just paint another number on it.

In 1963, Buck got a factory Pontiac deal and Neil saddled up Buck's old Chryslers numbered 86 and 88.

That was a Nichels Pontiac. That's the same Pontiac they were building in Spartanburg. I went to Nichels and picked up a brand-new Pontiac and brought it to Charlotte. We sent it over to Holman-Moody and had them put two roll bars in it that Nichels hadn't updated. I think in 1964 that's when Buddy went to 87. I believe some of those Chrysler 300s were number 86, too. So Baker made me a deal. "You helped me get them two Chevrolets out of Spartanburg and into the shop in Charlotte, so I'll sell you that other Chrysler 300 we got. I'll give you that Dodge you can tow it with and all you do is at the end of each race, if you make any money, give me a payment on it." I paid for that car a payment a race. Me and Baker got along. I went and did things like I wanted to do them and I said, "If you don't like it, say so." He trusted me because I bought that car on credit and never missed a payment on it. I bought both of his '62 Chryslers.

Neil had a good friend who was soon helping him chauffeur Buck's big Chryslers.

Jimmy Helms helped us work in the pits. Jimmy run an old short track sportsman car. Every time we went to the racetrack he wanted to go. So at

Darlington I had both of Buck's old Chryslers. We were going to run a qualifying race because that was my cup of tea. If there was a qualifying race, that was an extra $500 to start. If I started my car and the other car, that was $1,000 for that race. Jimmy never ran nothing except when we let him start the car and he got half the $500 and me or Baker got the other half. They got to where they named the race the Neil Castles Benefit. At Darlington, Jimmy said, "Let me start that car in the qualifying race." "OK," I said, "I'll tell you what. I'm going to lead it and you follow me, 'cause you're going to run second if I have to slow down and chance it." I led the race and with eight or ten laps to go, somebody got by him. I looked in the mirror and Jimmy wasn't behind me. So I just slowed down and let that guy go by and I got behind him. We run down in the corner and he couldn't stand the heat. Jimmy pulled up behind me and we finished one-two.

Suffice it to say, Neil eliminated the threat and Helms finished second in the "benefit" race. Driving Darlington in those days was much tougher than today. The Darlington Stripe you might pick up in turns three and four could be brutal on a car and nerve-wracking on its pilot.

The first thing was to go in on the bottom and who you were side by side with you were going to come out on his back bumper. Run him down that front straightaway and move him up into the rail. You'd get in the corner and it would accelerate so much better coming up out of that hole and she'd just slide on up there because them old tires just wouldn't stick. My theory was stay lower and drift up coming off so you'd already passed that damn corner. I did that to survive and to save the car.

The first race down there they put Slab Widenhouse in a Nash. We all laughed at it because it looked like an upside-down bathtub. Slab would just go down in the corner and bounce it off the rail and follow the rail. He wore that car down until there wasn't nothing left to scrape. There were a lot things that took place that many people didn't know. Some of those cars, not on mine, but some of the others, had two-by-twelves drove down inside the thing so if you'd get in the rail it would just slap the sheet metal up against it and go on. I didn't do it because we had good support with good roll cages on that side.

By the 1960s, many of the drivers and car owners had taken to the air to travel from home to the track and back. One particular driver was a professional corporate pilot, somewhat of a salesman, and a pretty scrappy driver.

Four. Racing into the '60s

J.T. Putney thought he was the greatest thing in the world as far as being a pilot went. Well, there was a landing strip behind that road course in Augusta, and Putney was trying to sell Cotton and David Pearson an airplane. He had a new twin-engine airplane that he was demonstrating and was going to land it on the strip beside the racetrack. He did a great job of landing it, but forgot one thing. He didn't put the landing gear down. They hit that runway and there went the props, the engines, it destroyed that plane.

At Asheville-Weaverville one time, it came a rainstorm in the middle of the race and we all got out and run and got in the back of our trucks to get out of the rain. I was in the back of my truck and somebody come running up there and yelled, "You better get down yonder. Buddy and Putney's in a fight and I don't know who's beating the hell out of who." I said, "Well, if Baker let's that little son of a bitch whip his ass, he needs it." But they did have a pretty good fist fight in the middle of the racetrack.

Somebody at that racetrack run into me one time, and hell, I was running in the top five. I cut a tire down and had to come in and change tires and I might as well have not even been there. I got back on the racetrack and the more I thought about it the madder I got. So I waited until he made a gas stop and when he stopped on pit road, I come off the racetrack and never took my foot off the gas. I went right through the back of him. I don't remember who it was, but I remember what the back of his car looked like after I hit it.

Back then, when you come out of the racetrack at Asheville-Weaverville right down that dirt road to get to the highway to Asheville, if you made a right turn, in that white house on the left was an old woman that was the biggest bootlegger in the county. Used to be when the race was over there was more cars parked at her house than at the racetrack. But for fighting at the track, Pat Purcell, field manager and vice president of NASCAR, sent out a letter to NASCAR competitors that said, "At this time there will be no more holes shot in cars during competition." There was a lot of drivers that carried a gun in the racecar. I carried a one-inch socket and a pull handle to change the torsion bar on the left side when there wasn't anybody looking. But I don't know what happened a little earlier to prompt that letter.

The third race of the 1964 season took place on Sunday, December 1, 1963, at Speedway Park on a rough, rutted, poorly kept half-mile dirt track in Jacksonville, Florida. It would turn out to be one of the most significant races in NASCAR history and nobody realized it for years. Neil Castles started 17th in his 1962 Chrysler number 86 right behind African-American driver Wendell Scott, inside of Ed Livingston, and just ahead of Johnny Allen.

That old racetrack was made out of oil and sand. Me and Baker had two cars there. We loaded up the radiator with that old oil and sand. We were there washing the radiator out. Buck had a big screen on the front of his and kept the dirt out better than I did. They said that Baker won the race and gave him the trophy. After that, Johnny Bruner decided Wendell Scott was the winner. Wendell came down there standing in the pit road and said, "Buck, you gots to go up there and kiss that woman. I can't do that. I want the money, but I'm not going over there." Buck was second. Wendell and I got along. We had our ups and downs, but I got along pretty good with Wendell. They hired me to do that movie, *Greased Lightning*, and up until then Wendell was just one of the bunch. His wife Mary and Jean sat on the scorer's stand together. But at Jacksonville, we just did the best we could and got out of there. Everybody was pacing, slowing down, and trying to wash out their radiators.

As it has grown in legend and lore, Wendell Scott's win in his old beat-up Ned Jarrett hand-me-down Chevy was a watermark in the history of NASCAR as the first, and so far only, win by an African American driver. As hard as NASCAR tried to hinder Scott's racing effort, when he had it right, he was hard to handle. Not only did Wendell win the 200-lapper that day, he actually ran 202 laps to second-place Buck Baker's 200. Third that day was Jack Smith, fourth Ed Livingston, fifth Richard Petty, and sixth Neil Castles.

The Fifth Annual World 600 was held on Sunday, May 24, 1964, at the Charlotte Motor Speedway. Buck Baker was in a Ray Fox factory Dodge, and his pair of 1962 Chryslers were there with Neil in the number 86 he was driving (and buying) and Jimmy Helms in the number 88. It was another tragic race.

Junior Johnson and Ned Jarrett got to banging on each other and Fireball was in the midst of it. I was about three or four cars back. Fireball spun that Holman-Moody Ford and hit the inside wall backwards and turned into a ball of fire. I went on by and when I come back around they had the caution flag out. Ned Jarrett had got Fireball out of the car 'cause he was trying to drag him away from the fire when I went by. On the next lap by, they red-flagged the race. Ralph Moody's wife was a nurse and she went to the hospital every day to take care of Fireball. Fireball's wife Doris even stayed at Moody's house over on Park Road in Charlotte. In the meantime, I'd already took my car and

Four. Racing into the '60s

Wendell Scott prepares to back his racer off the trailer at Columbia Speedway on April 8, 1971 (Perry Allen Wood Racing Archives).

went to Daytona. Fireball died the day we qualified at Daytona. I called Jean and told her to get my suit and everything, package it up, and send it to me.

Fireball Roberts fought for his life until passing away on July 2, 1964, in Charlotte, Neil's hometown. Neil needed his suit to attend Fireball's funeral in Daytona Beach, Fireball's hometown. It was the funeral of a friend he had known for over a decade, since they were practically roommates at Leland Colvin's house in Camden building modifieds and hauling tobacco to Winston-Salem. They were old friends; good friends. Neil Castles finished 38th in the 600 in his two-year-old Chrysler, bringing home $650. Fireball Roberts' purple Holman-Moody Ford finished 35th and his widow Doris got $650 as well. With the passing of Buddy Shuman in 1955 and Fireball Roberts nine years later, Neil had lost two of the people involved in racing closest to him.

To start the 1965 season, Buck Baker added a used car to his stable, which Neil drove frequently.

We got a Dodge that Buck had bought from Cotton Owens. I put it on the truck and took it to California for Buck to run the Riverside race in. Buck bought

Neil "Soapy" Castles

that car for himself to run Riverside and finished ninth. In the meantime, Buck had got that new Oldsmobile deal. He had the Oldsmobile at Daytona and there was a big crash in the qualifying race and I was right in the middle of it coming off the fourth corner. When I passed Buck, he was sitting in the racetrack in his seat. The seat came out of the car and he was sitting in the seat with his seat belt on in the middle of the racetrack. We had to put 88 on that Dodge because we had 86 on the Plymouth and 87 on the new Oldsmobile.

And a strong car it was, serving Buck's team well. Neil and the Dodge took fifth on the Fourth of July in the Firecracker 400 at Daytona Beach, along with three other top tens.

An annual ritual of the Grand National circuit from about 1957 until it died on the vine after Winston took over in 1972 was the summertime Northern Tour. Its venues changed over the years, but basically included stops at various times at tracks in Pennsylvania, New Jersey, New York, Connecticut, and Maine.

A stellar performance in the 1965 Firecracker 400 at Daytona International Speedway saw Neil Castles start 24th and finish fifth in an unheralded year-old Dodge from the Buck Baker stable (Neil Castles Family Collection).

Four. Racing into the '60s

Often the teams literally caravanned their way up the eastern seaboard on Interstates where available, and nearly always on narrow back roads. Neil Castles remembers it well, as the following years of recollections reflect. The first took place at Watkins Glen International Raceway in Watkins Glen, New York, prior to the race on Sunday, July 19, 1964.

> We qualified and the transmission come out of the Chrysler 300 and I didn't have another transmission. There wasn't one there, but there was one at the shop. So we went over to the office at the racetrack and called and I had them put that transmission on an airplane and send it to Jersey City, New Jersey, pick up on arrival. Me and Jean took a pickup truck and ran 100 miles an hour all the way through New York State to get to the airport. I got that transmission and threw it in the back of the truck and flew back to the racetrack. I left the car on jack stands, and when we got back there I just slid under it and slid that transmission in there, put four bolts in it, put the cross member in, stuck the drive shaft in it, and let the jack down just in time to push it to the line.

That shows how badly Neil Castles wanted to race. Not just this race, but any race.

A pair of notable events took place that day. Billy Wade in Bud Moore's Mercury Marauder won his fourth consecutive race, which had never been done before, even during the Kiekhaefer years. Also, Neil started 18th in 1962 Chrysler number 88 just behind Doug Moore, to the right of Doug Cooper, and just ahead of Lee Petty. Over 16 years, Papa Lee started 427 races beginning with Strictly Stock Car Race Number 1, where he crashed, bringing out the first caution flag ever in what is today the Monster Energy Cup Series. From 1949 to 1961 he won at least one race every year, 54 in all, and three Grand National Championships. Sunday, July 19, 1964, he raced for the last time ever.

On the Northern Tour, Neil and his fellow travelers found that all the hazards were not always on the speedways.

> All of us pretty well traveled together. We were in Bridgehampton, Long Island, New York. When the race was over with, the promoter, Lou Figari, had made arrangements to have the ferry pick us up on the other side of the island and take us right straight across the channel. We were to get off and go to the racetrack in Old Bridge, New Jersey. They had us and the Bakers reservations in a motel and we all went to our rooms and the place was a fleabag. It wasn't nothing decent to stay in. Baker came over there and knocked on the door and

said, "Have you taken a shower?" "Hell no. I ain't that brave." He said, "Well, don't try it." You'd go in the bathroom and there was a pipe sticking out of the wall and you turn on the spigot and the water would shoot clear across the room. We stayed there until daylight and went in the restaurant. Me, Jean, Buck, and Margaret sat down to eat. They brought this food out there and it looked like junk. About that time the owner of the motel came up and said, "We've got this bill here that you're going to have to take care of." He said it was going to be so many thousands of dollars and this, that, and the other. Buck said, "How in the hell did you come up with that?" The manager said, "Well, one thing about it, you came in last night. That's $1,000. You're here today, that's the next day. That's $2,000. You owe $4,000 right now, plus the food." Baker looked at me and said, "Neil, give me some money." I reached in my pocket and gave him some change. "I'm going to go over there and put it in that pay phone, call the damn police, and tell them to get out here 'cause I'm going to kill this son of a bitch right here in the floor." Lou Figari had told that manager we were rich race drivers and all he had to do was take care of us. $4,000! You come in at night and wake up in the morning and it's another day. By the time the police got there, we just got up and walked out the door. The hell with it.

There may not have been a more volatile individual to try to take advantage of than Buck Baker. The innkeeper got off lucky. Many others did not.
The time and location of the following incident is difficult to pinpoint, but is another example of Neil's relationship with Wendell Scott.

I was running damn good, up front. I came off the fourth corner and that damn Wendell Scott was sitting right in the middle of the racetrack dead still and I hit him right in the back end. It busted the radiator, naturally. Well, Bill France pitched a fit that I ran over Wendell on purpose. All the NAACP people said that because he was black I ran over him on purpose. They had a big stink about the white guy running over the black guy 'cause he was black. France got his nose in it. After that, a month or two later, Wendell came over and said, "Neil, I didn't aim to start all that mess up there. I didn't want to have nothing to do with that, the NAACP bunch, or nothing else. I didn't ever tell you, but I ran out of gas. That's the reason I stopped in front of you. I wouldn't have done it for nothing in the world." Well, Buck had a fit. "What in the hell did you have to run over him for?" We were on the Northern Tour, so I went to the dealership in the next town, Watkins Glen, went to the body shop, and found enough parts to fix it.

Four. Racing into the '60s

Neil and Wendell crossed paths constantly and much has been written about it. There appears to have been a mutual respect between the two hardworking, hard-driving competitors.

Risking bodily injury never seemed to slow Neil Castles down very much, as was witnessed in a melting-hot pit area on Long Island one blazing summer day on the Northern Tour. The date is uncertain. Neil's springing into action to help somebody in trouble is very certain.

We went to Islip, New York, to a little quarter-mile racetrack and all of us parked side by side in the infield near the pits. This is in the summertime and it's hotter than Hell. John Sears parked right beside me. John jacked that old car up, put jack stands under it, and he's going to change the gear. He slid under there and changed the damn gear and the jack stands sunk into that asphalt. I jumped out of the pickup and hollered for everybody on pit road to come help me. We picked that car up off John and I slid under the car, some of them got my feet, and I pulled him back from underneath the rear end. They held the car up until we got out from under it. Well, those jack stands just sunk in that hot asphalt. So, nobody got hurt, but that was a very exciting situation with John under that car.

Every time John Sears had to go to the bathroom, they'd come get me to drive the car if I was out of the race. John was a lot bigger than I was. All I had to do was tie two or three knots in the seat belt and hold on.

John had that old Ford and L.G. DeWitt let him have new Ford. I ran it at Charlotte and was behind Richard Petty when he blew a right rear tire and spun. The next lap I blew a right rear tire and spun right behind him. I damn near blew all the sheet metal out of the right side of the car. After the race was over, me and Richard walked over there to see what we ran over. Somebody had blown a clutch out of a car [and] one of the discs out of it was sticking out of the racetrack just like a razor blade. I took my pair of vise grips and pulled it out of the asphalt.

It is obvious that there was very little that Neil would not do to help out Big John Sears, a man of enormous dimensions.

Once again, Neil Castles was able to apply his midget training to the big stockers.

I liked that old road course at Watkins Glen. I found me a home place where you could dive down in the corner and drift up on the wall, come back

Lifting the Olds' right front wheel, Neil Castles powers through a right-hander with one hand on July 10, 1966, at Bridgehampton Raceway, Bridgehampton, New York (Neil Castles Family Collection).

down in the corner, and you could pass two cars in the corner. I changed the springs and shocks on that Oldsmobile and went back to the midgets. I was picking the right front up tire. Putting the weight on the left front and driving the car with the left front tire. That way I could dive down in the corner, get on the gas, drift up to the wall, and still have plenty of right front to keep from hitting the wall. I learned from some of the best. Bill Shockley was an ace in a midget and I learned things from him.

The Northern Tour is always discussed by the people fortunate enough to have experienced it. It was a nomadic life in which competitors beat each other to pieces on the tracks, but in between, traveled as one and defended each other as one. Everybody had his neighbor's back and it appears to be a long-lost phenomenon of current stock car racing. Too bad.

Five

Elvis Is in the Building

As seems to be the case with all those involved in racing in the early days when flat towing was more the norm and trailering rare, cars got away, and frequently with amusing results. One happened returning home from a race.

I was following Buddy Baker home from Spartanburg and we got off at Wilkinson Boulevard and turned to go up to the shop behind the airport. Buddy was towing a Dodge that he had wrecked with J.T. Putney that night. Buddy and J.T. didn't get along very well. It followed two or three other instances. Anyway, Buddy went flying around a damn corner, turned, and the racecar went straight. The car came loose, sailed down through a yard, and hit a house. Well, I pulled over and got stopped over in front of the neighbor's house. I ran back there to see what was going on. Buddy said, "I got to get out of here before Daddy finds out what happened. He's going to kill us!" I said, "Well, there ain't much way to get out of it." The old man that owned the house was out there and had already called all the police in town. He was demanding the insurance and he wanted all this shit and that the racecar was valuable and all that was going on. I just slid into the seat of the racecar and cranked it up, backed it out of the driveway, drove it over the shop at the airport and parked it. The others were out there arguing who was going to fix the house. The guy that worked in the engine room at the shop brought me back to get my racecar. I came back and got in my truck, eased out of there, and took it to the shop and put the car in the garage. By then, they decided that Buddy's insurance would cover the damage to the house and he came to the shop. But they were holding the car that damaged the house for the insurance people. Then they got around to finding out they didn't have the damn car. They never did figure out how that car left there.

How in the world Neil pulled that off is incredible. Apparently Neil and the racecar were quicker and tougher than the old man and his house. But Neil was not through. He lost one himself with even more amazing results.

I lost the Oldsmobile. I left the shop with John, Jean's brother, and was coming to the house to get my clothes and then go on to Occoneechee Speedway in Hillsborough. I got to the house and my car was gone. Buck's Oldsmobile was on the truck, but my tow bar came loose and my Oldsmobile was gone. We called the police. We searched every inch of the road from the shop to the house. There was no sign of that car ever coming loose and being gone. So I called Buck and he said, "Well, you got my car on the truck. Just take it on and drive my car tomorrow. I don't need to go no damn way."

I got back from Hillsborough and went to the shop. The people at the Ford warehouse had called and said there was a racecar parked in their lot and they don't know how we got it in there. What happened was that, there where you turn to go to the airport on Wilkinson Boulevard on the right side, we came across that railroad bridge above Ford and that car came loose crossing that railroad bridge, come right down there and got in that grass, turned, and when it hit the chain-link fence, the front end was low and it just went under the chain-link fence, went down the hill, and set down right between two new Fords in that parking lot. There was no sign of that car ever going in that parking lot. It just went under that chain-link fence. That's why we couldn't see it.

These incredible events appear to have taken place surrounding the running of the 1966 Joe Weatherly 150 on Sunday, September 18. That day Neil Castles started 11th and recorded a seventh-place finish. Buck Baker's name was not listed among the participants.

The year 1965 was not a whole lot better than 1964 as far as NASCAR fatalities were concerned. Neil Castles shed some light on a couple late in the season. The first was on Monday, September 6, 1965, at Darlington Raceway during the Southern 500.

This guy named Smitty handled all of the Pure Oil products everywhere and kept a list of how many cars got gas, filled up our cans during the race, who got oil, everything to do with Union Oil. He kept up with seeing that all the drivers got what they were allocated for. During the race everybody was running back to get cans of gas from him for the pit stops. Now, Peggy was Smitty's wife and had an old bus and in the back of that bus she had a sewing machine. She made me a brand-new red uniform for that race. In the meantime, she made another one just like it for Buren Skeen. Well, when they crashed down in the corner and got Buren Skeen out and laid him down in the racetrack

Five. Elvis Is in the Building

in that red uniform, everybody thought it was me and they announced I got killed. Jean is a witness to the fact. I've still got that uniform in my basement.

The T-bone crash took the life of rookie Buren Skeen in a race in which he and Neil wore red uniforms made by the same lady before the race. Neil and Jean Castles' basement holds that uniform, along with enough racing artifacts and photographs to be a museum all its own.

In the very next major race on Sunday, October 17, 1965, at Charlotte Motor Speedway, the National 400 was held and Harold Kite, an old-timer, met a similar T-bone fate.

Harold had come home from the Army. He stayed in the Army for years. Him and Curtis Turner were good friends. He was going to build a new racecar. When they were qualifying they needed a gear, and I loaned them a gear for that car he got killed in.

Neil Castles does not like to talk about death or racing people being killed. He does because he's been surrounded by it and defied enough for several lifetimes. The passing of more than 50 years have no doubt erased a lot of the bad in his mind. Harold Kite died when hit by Jimmy Helms, Neil's teammate in Buck Baker's old Chrysler days.

Like a chess player, Neil tried to think several moves ahead. He did it in a racecar and it probably kept him safe.

There's things that drivers went by. If I'm running at Charlotte or any superspeedway, especially at Daytona, when you come off the number-two corner, the car's going to drift to the wall anyway. As soon as you get leveled off two, start looking. If you see smoke on the third and fourth corner over there, you better start slowing down 'cause you're going to hit a pile of shit shortly. The main thing was to look for the tire smoke to see where the next wreck was before you got to it.

On Friday, May 13, 1966, at Starlite Speedway in Monroe, North Carolina, a rare breed of race was run: an all-independent event. It was not intended to be that way, but for some reason or another, there were no factory cars in sight. It was a rainy evening when Neil saddled up Buck's most reliable car in ninth place on the grid right behind J.T. Putney's Chevy, inside of Clyde Lynn's Ford, and just ahead of J.D. McDuffie's Ford.

I took that 1965 Plymouth number 86 to Starlite Speedway and qualified well and the old car run good. I had led the race most of the night. It got down close to the end and I stopped to get gas during the last caution flag. It got down to ten or 15 laps to go and Johnny Bruner, Jr., started motioning me to go to the pits. I'm leading the race and he's motioning me to go to the pits. I ain't going! It got down to seven or eight laps to go and he got out his black flag and started waving the black flag at me. Then Buck and them came out on the side of the racetrack telling me, "Come on over here and stop! Come on over here and stop!" I got to where I'd go into the corner and the ass end of the old car would get loose and slide right up the hill and I'd get back in it. The old car just worked good. Every once in a while it would make a hell of a racket like the rear end was coming out from under it. It would come down the racetrack and I'd throw it in the corner. It got down to four laps to go and they demanded that I stop. Getting out on the racetrack and everything. I came down the damn pit road and stopped. They threw the deck lid up, shut the deck lid down, and motioned me to go on. So I went from the lead to wherever I finished, but I was leading the race when I went into the pits. What happened was that when we were lined up to start the race, somebody had left a nitrogen bottle in the trunk of the car. Every time that thing would get sliding sideways, it'd throw it sideways a little more. Finally the bottle was sticking out of the quarter panel of the car about so far. I knew there was something going on back there. I'd hear something slam around back there. I did finish fourth. That was the first car that NASCAR approved to put a hemi engine in.

The top five for the 250-lapper on the half-mile of dirt were Darel Dieringer, Clyde Lynn, Wendell Scott, Neil, and Henley Gray. This was the third in a stretch of five consecutive races in a brutal 15 days. Neil Castles drove that trusty old hemi to a third in Hampton, Virginia; fifth at Macon, Georgia; fourth at Monroe; seventh at Richmond, Virginia; and then came the marathon World 600 at Charlotte.

The World 600 on Sunday, May 22, 1966, in Charlotte, was arguably the best day Buck Baker's mismatched collection of racecars ever had. In the longest race of the year, Buck's stable came home fifth with Neil in the Oldsmobile number 87, sixth was Paul Connors in the two-year-old Dodge now numbered 86, and Buck himself was tenth in a new Chevelle number 88. Neil's race that hot Sabbath was epic.

Five. Elvis Is in the Building

Neil Castles in the pits during the World 600 on May 28, 1966, at Charlotte Motor Speedway. After Neil's windshield was smashed out by flying debris, racer Darel Dieringer on his right provided a motel towel to shield Neil's face (Neil Castles Collection).

I was in a line of traffic and something came off a car and cars started going everywhere. Then it hit my windshield on the right side of the car. I realized what was happening and got out of the line of traffic 'cause I didn't want to crash in another wreck. I came down pit road and Kenneth Rice, who was working for us, jumped the pit wall and grabbed the windshield that was inside the car on the right side, shoved it out the front on the hood, and pulled it off. While I'm sitting there, Darel Dieringer had an old motel towel and he crammed it in my shirt and over my mouth and nose. They took a roll of gray tape and run around it and I couldn't see. I had a pair of them old bubble goggles and I couldn't see nothing out of them. So I wiped them with that towel and run a piece of gray tape across the top and bottom of them and went back out there. The worst problem I had was passing. Every time I'd get out from behind a car, the pressure on my chest was so great I couldn't get my breath. I couldn't get any air. I'd catch myself trying to pull that towel up there so I could breathe through it to get some air. I won enough for us to eat on for a week.

Jean and Neil likely ate for more than a week as Neil soldiered under the checkers 29 laps behind in a 400-lap race, winning $3,440. In a very high-attrition race of enormous length, 29 laps behind in fifth was quite a feat. Consider the lack of a windshield for about the last third of the race with only a flimsy pair of plastic goggles between him and whatever else might fly up off the track, as well as the breathing difficulty he was having. I was at that race as a 14-year-old, and now in my 60-plus years of following all forms of the sport since I've seen few events that equal the pure courage and determination Neil Castles displayed that long, hot afternoon. An amazing feat it was in the face of incredible odds. NASCAR would no more let you continue like Neil did that day than they would give away free tickets. The photo of Neil Castles peering straight ahead through fragile plastic goggles out where a windshield used to be is an image for the ages. Add to that the facts of no window safety net as they have today, no gloves as Neil's bare right hand is visible on the gear shift, no head and neck restraint, no headrest, no radio, and no full-face helmet. Neil Castles is truly the face of courage.

A rather unfortunate occurrence took place on the way home from a race one evening, and as always, Neil did what he could to help.

One time after the Darlington race, me and Jean loaded up and were coming back to Charlotte. Up there at Hartsville, South Carolina, at that big crossroads coming up 74, somebody up ahead of us got tied up on that intersection towing a damn racecar and I don't know who hit who first, but he wrecked a truckload of bricks and a person got killed. I drove up there about the time all that was going on and got out and went over there and started talking to him. He said, "I don't know what to do." Well, this old police [officer] was standing there running his mouth and I went over there and talked to him. Everything around there was controlled by Bob Colvin. If you needed it done, Bob could get it done. Bob owned the Darlington Raceway. This state patrolman lived in Darlington and was at the racetrack all the time just hanging out. I said, "Well, look, call Bob and tell him that this guy's a good friend of mine and we got a problem and we need it to go away." The patrolman said, "Take that man and that racecar and tell him to follow you to Charlotte and it never happened." So I brought him to Charlotte. He immediately sold that racecar to Holman and Moody.

Five. Elvis Is in the Building

Staring straight ahead through where the windshield used to be, Neil Castles is the epitome of courage. Wearing flimsy goggles and no gloves, Neil soldiered on, finishing an incredible fifth place in the World 600 on May 28, 1966 (Neil Castles Family Collection).

It is unknown whether Holman and Moody was aware of what that racecar had been involved with earlier. The fact is that it did not stick around their shop very long, and again Neil played a hand in the action.

Holman and Moody were going to run in some races in Australia. So Holman had to send so many cars down there. He bought that racecar and sent it to Australia. They had to take the car to New Orleans to catch the ship to Australia and ain't got nobody that can get to New Orleans quick enough. John Holman wanted to talk to me. I went over there and John said, "Can you get that car down there to catch that ship?" I said, "Yeah, where's it at?" "Down in the shop." It was raining and I went down there and said, "Get the windshield wipers and lights working on it and I'll drive the damn thing down there and catch me an airplane home." He said, "Well, we need to take two cars. Would you tow another one behind that one?" "Yeah." So I hooked another racecar behind the first one. He told me when I was done to have somebody box up the tow bar and send it back to me C.O.D. I unhooked the cars down there in New Orleans at midnight and checked in the motel and slept three or four hours. I got up and got me an airplane flight out of there about six in the morning. I come back to Charlotte and there were a few people who couldn't understand how I could get two cars to New Orleans overnight in a rainstorm. They wanted to know how I could see where I was going. I said I bought two cases of Coca-Cola and poured it on the windshield and the wipers kept it clean as a whistle. Then John called me and said, "I got my tow bar back from them son-of-a-bitches and they charged so much to ship it that I could have bought four more." "You said to ship it to you and I did."

A racecar with a somewhat checkered past was banished to racetracks 10,000 miles away to fade into the shadows of history.
When 1967 rolled around, Neil got into the Daytona 500 rather unexpectedly in a car that needed a driver. The results were outstanding.

We got to Daytona and they didn't have enough cars to run the ARCA [Automobile Racing Club of America] race. Somebody from NASCAR went over and got Emory Gilliam who was running his 00 Plymouth in the Daytona 500 after the ARCA. He said, "Get Neil to run that car in the ARCA race and soon as the race is over I'll pull you right straight from the ARCA garage area into our area. We'll run your car through NASCAR inspection and you'll be ready to run the next week." So I come over there and run the ARCA race because they didn't have enough cars. There was a big fuss between Bill France [NASCAR] and John Marcum [ARCA] anyway. It was always a cut-throat deal.

Well, in the ARCA race with a lap and a half to go, I blowed the damn engine leading the race. It was a pretty decent-looking old car. Goldsmith thought that this was an opportunity to have a Chrysler car up front. He was just helping me, but he was working for Chrysler and he wanted to see that Plymouth win that race. And I did, too.

There wasn't no such thing as a crew chief. We just all helped each other. So they went to work in the pits and we done the chassis on it, got it set up where I could just run it where I wanted it to and it felt good. Every once in a while Goldsmith would hold up a pit board with a number and an arrow

Five. Elvis Is in the Building

on it. That told me either who was just ahead or right behind. They'd hold up a pit board that said, "GAS." You had to pit on the laps you were required to. If they put out a caution, you knew you could just drop in there and pit. But you had to watch that pit board. They had that tower in the infield that told you where you were running all the time. Long as I could see that double zero leading the race, I didn't have to worry. All I had to do was wait for them to tell me, "Come in here and get gas," and we had it played down to the last lap and the engine blowed.

The record shows that Neil started the number 00 in second place and led for 23 laps, blowing with 15 laps to go. That two-year-old Plymouth was obviously a good car and Neil at the helm made for a potent combination. But the motor was shot, and a much bigger prize was awaiting at the end of 500 more miles.

The next morning Gil didn't have ten cents to his name and I went over to Bill France, Jr.'s, office. I said, "Do you have any connections to help me get an engine for that car? I need to put an engine in it today." He said,

In a last-minute ride, Neil led often before blowing the engine and nearly winning the ARCA 250 at Daytona on February 19, 1967. One week later he brought the same underdog Plymouth home to an amazing tenth in the Daytona 500 (Neil Castles Family Collection).

Neil "Soapy" Castles

"NASCAR does not get involved in helping any drivers fix a car. If it's broke, you go fix it." I said, "Well, OK." That was just Billy, Jr. Old Man France was good and his wife Annie was nice.

One time I was in Daytona and Jean was coming to meet me and I was staying at the Days Inn or somewhere. Jean got there late or early or something and couldn't find out where I was at. So Jean called NASCAR and Bill France sent somebody over there and got her and took over to their house to spend the night. They sent her to the motel the next morning. But Billy, Jr., wasn't much help.

Gil finally was able to borrow an engine from somebody, I don't remember who, and went out and ran great in the Daytona 500. That old car just handles so good that we wound up in tenth.

After a so-so qualifying race, Neil lined up 26th on the grid and got that old hemi humming. When Mario Andretti took the checkers in a shocking upset, Neil Castles had pulled off a mild one of his own. He brought the red with yellow numeraled Gilliam Automotive Plymouth 00 home nine laps behind the winner in tenth place! He was a lap behind Jim Hurtubise's new factory-backed Norm Nelson Plymouth and five ahead of Donnie Allison's Chevelle. Imagine how it could have been if the engine had held together in the ARCA race. Neil definitely got the most out of what he had to work with during Speed Weeks 1967.

I was also at the World 600 the next year after the windshield incident, which was held on a scorching Sunday, May 28, 1967. Neil was immersed in the filming of the Metro-Goldwyn-Mayer (MGM) production of Speedway *starring Elvis Presley and Nancy Sinatra with direction by 1931 Academy Award winner Norman Taurog. Taurog took Oscar home as Best Director for* Skippy, *which starred Jackie Cooper. He was also nominated again in 1938 for* Boys Town. *Taurog started directing movies in 1920 before they learned to talk and his resume includes* Huckleberry Finn, The Adventures of Tom Sawyer, The Wizard of Oz *(uncredited),* Young Tom Edison, *several Martin and Lewis movies, and most of Presley's latter efforts.* Speedway *was to be the 69-year-old legend's penultimate motion picture. After Neil agreed to make* Speedway *with MGM, he needed to get a racecar.*

I went to see Richard Howard and told him I had a movie offer coming up and I needed to buy a new racecar. I had to have enough money to buy a racecar and I needed it before the Charlotte race because I was going to do a movie with MGM. I had already agreed to do the movie *Speedway* and they

Five. Elvis Is in the Building

agreed to pay me $5,000 to do it. I asked Richard if he'd give me $5,000 to buy the car. He said, "I'll make you a deal. I'll give you $5,000, you buy the car, and I'll put whoever's name on that car for the race I want." OK, he gave me the $5,000 to buy the car and he put [the name of] an insurance company on that car for the race. He and somebody else owned an insurance company together. Well, he put the name of that insurance company on there so he could deduct the $5,000 on his taxes. He gave me the money and I went straight to Cotton Owens and gave it to him for a Dodge that same day. I brought the car home and that was car I used to do *Speedway* with Elvis and Nancy Sinatra. I gave Richard the $5,000 back and he got paid for putting that insurance company name on the car. He pretty well collected double on that deal. I raced that car the rest of the year.

A line in Neil Castles' May 11, 1967, MGM contract states: "In the performance of your services hereunder you shall act as a driver of said Racing Car in said race and shall also, to such extent as we desire, act as a photographic double for Elvis Presley and /or others." I mean, that line alone is worth the $5,000 he was paid by the giant of all Hollywood studios. And the insurance company was The Walker Agency. The Internet has multiple insurance agencies by that name now from coast to coast. The Walker Agency that graced the quarter panels of Neil's Dodge for the making of Speedway *has long since gone out of business and none of the current agencies were connected to it in any way.*

It was May of 1967 and Neil Castles is home in Charlotte making a racing movie with MGM starring Elvis Presley and Nancy Sinatra directed by Academy Award winner Norman Taurog. Not bad!

I had my own 1965 Dodge number 06 and made the deck lid where you could move the camera anywhere you wanted to on the back. Right beside me I had all my sound stuff and a camera mounted on what you'd call a tray. Part of this is still down yonder in the shop. This camera would swivel where you could get the grandstand. What they wanted was to film the people in the grandstand when they dropped the green flag. On the other camera they wanted to be able to see the cars taking off down the front straightaway when they dropped the green flag. That was the first car that was approved to run a camera in NASCAR. I also had the first non-usable pit stall when you came off the racetrack at turn four. That's where I stopped to change film, changed all my sound track, changed everything. This movie has got two race drivers in it, but they've only got one car in the actual race. So they can't have a

METRO-GOLDWYN-MAYER INC.
10202 West Washington Blvd.
Culver City, California

May 11, 1967

Mr. H. Neil Castles
4216 McKinley Drive
Charlotte, N. C.

Dear Mr. Castles:

You warrant to us that you are the sole owner of that certain Stock Car racing automobile know as a Dodge 1965, hereinafter called the Racing Car.

We have advised you that we desire to photograph and record that certain stock car race known as the "Eighth Annual "World 600"" which is to take place at the Charlotte Motor Speedway on May 28, 1967 or, in event of inclement weather, June 4, 1967.

For this purpose you agree to cause said Racing Car described above to be entered in said race and to be modified to our satisfaction by the installation of camera mounts so that motion picture of said race can be photographed from said Racing Car prior to, during and after said race.

You agree to furnish said Racing Car for said purpose with you as the driver thereof. In addition to furnishing said Racing Car and your own services, you are to furnish necessary mechanics and other members of a pit crew of competent and experienced persons to service said Racing Car during period of this agreement. You are also to furnish all fuel, entry fees and maintenance of said Racing Car. The camera and camera equipment to be mounted on said Racing Car and the film therefore are to be furnished by us.

It is understood that our obligations hereunder are subject to your qualifying said Racing Car to enter said race and you agree to use your best efforts to so qualify it.

In the performance of your services hereunder you shall act as driver of said Racing Car in said race and shall also, to such extent as we desire, act as a photographic double for Elvis Presley and/or others.

Provided that you fully perform all of your obligations and agreements hereunder; that said Racing Car qualifies and participates in said race and that you cooperate with us and assist us to the fullest extent reasonably possible, we agree to pay you the sum of Five Thousand Dollars ($5,000.00) upon the completion of all of your services hereunder. All compensation of your mechanics, pit crew and other persons engaged by you shall be paid by you and you agree to hold us harmless from and against any and all claims for compensation payable to any of them.

You agree that we, our successors, licensees and assigns shall own all rights of every kind in and to all photographs and/or recordings made by us in connection herewith and in and to all other results and proceeds of your services, including the right to use the same, all or in part, in such manner as we may desire, without limitation or restriction of any kind.

Page one of Neil Castles' MGM contract. Paragraph six states that he will "act as a photographic double for Elvis Presley and/or others" for $5,000 (next paragraph) (Neil Castles Family Collection).

second driver. They had to have a second driver in this race at the same time. So I set up these camera locations. I came down pit road, jumped out of the car, took off a uniform, put on another uniform, changed helmets, changed everything, jumped back in the car and I was the second driver. So that movie only had one driver. Me.

Five. Elvis Is in the Building

Neil and an MGM technician to his right secure a camera to the deck lid of his racecar during the filming of *Speedway* in May of 1967 at the Charlotte Motor Speedway (Neil Castles Family Collection).

In the pits before a packed World 600 grandstand on May 28, 1967, at the Charlotte Motor Speedway, Neil changes uniforms during the filming of *Speedway*. By doing so he can be filmed driving for both the parts of stars Elvis Presley and Ross Hagen (Neil Castles Family Collection).

Five. Elvis Is in the Building

Elvis Presley and Neil played the role of Steve Grayson and drove Cotton Owens' 1967 Dodge Charger number 6 that was actually driven to third place in the race by Bobby Allison. Grayson/Presley wore a white uniform with blue stripes down the sleeves and a silver helmet. Ross Hagen and Neil played the role of Grayson's chief adversary Paul Dado, who drove Richard Petty's number 43 Plymouth, which actually finished fourth. Hagen/Dado wore a white uniform with red stripes down the sleeves and a white helmet.

That was actually Cotton's Dodge we used. I paid him $10,000 for that car. He wanted $10,000 cash and I took it down there in the back and handed it to him. Every car I ever bought from Cotton he wanted cash. That old black truck he sold me, he didn't want to sell it, but he'd sell it to me if I'd bring him cash. I took the money down there to Spartanburg to him and drove it back. He called me two or three years later and wanted to buy it back. I said, "Well, Cotton, I gave you $10,000 for it, I'll take $8,000 for it back." "Oh, you're crazy as hell. I wouldn't give you a dime for it," and hung up on me.

Neil crashed Cotton's car in an extremely authentic accident where he crosses the finish line in a qualifying attempt, slides across the grass between

The camera car Neil Castles drove during the filming of *Speedway*. The movie paid for the racecar and Richard Howard had his insurance and furniture companies sponsor it (Neil Castles Family Collection).

the track and the pits, and slams violently into the pit wall backwards. The entire sequence is captured on film and is quite exciting. He also bounces his obsolete old Chrysler number 88 off the guardrail between turns three and four. This time, he did not mingle with stars Elvis Presley, Nancy Sinatra, or Bill Bixby.

I met Elvis just briefly. We were in and out of the business office. I signed some papers and I was gone. The director was Norman Taurog. I have a full-page letter he wrote to me thanking me for that show.

That letter dated June 27, 1967, thanks Neil for his assistance in the making of Speedway *and has the added handwritten "PS Say Hi to my Private Indian."*

An unidentified assistant on the far left watches as director Norman Taurog looks to throw a punch, with Nancy Sinatra and Elvis Presley on the far right looking on while filming *Speedway* (Neil Castles Family Collection).

Five. Elvis Is in the Building

That is a reference to Neil's Native American friend Roy Tyner, who helped with some of the driving in the movie. He is not included in the IMDb listing.

And what is very strange about the IMDb coverage of Speedway is that for all Neil's involvement with the stunt work and technical innovations and being Elvis' double, he gets no mention at all either. Stunts list Carey Loftin and five others, all noted as uncredited, and the cast names Richard Petty,

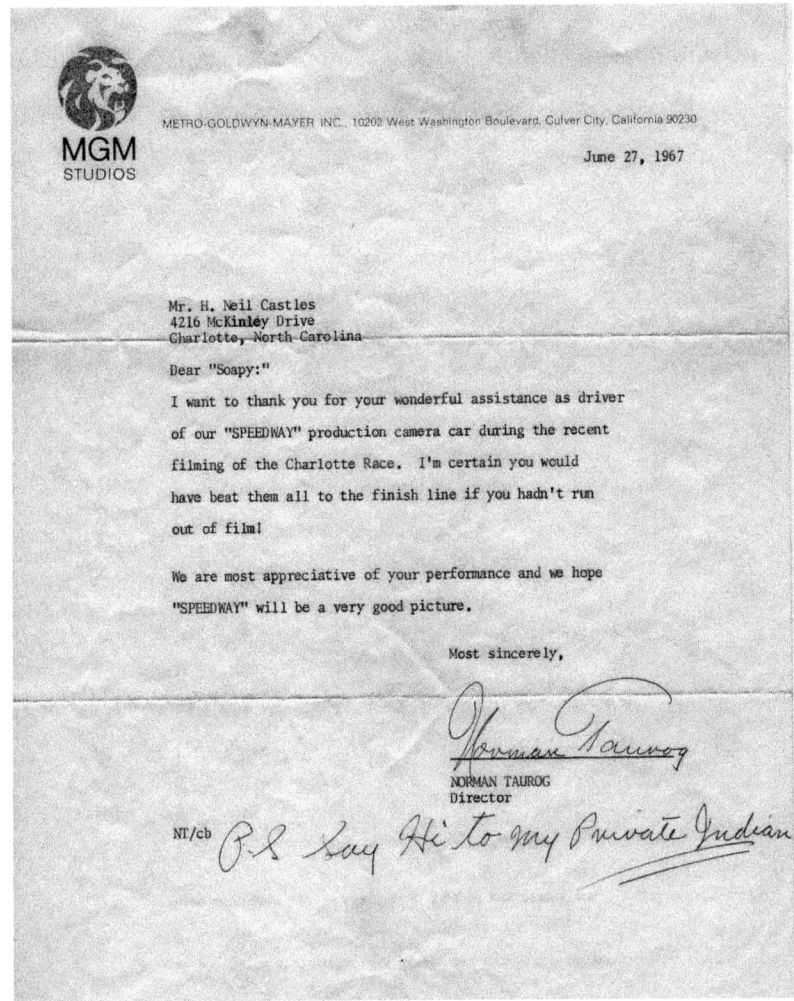

Thank-you letter from director Norman Taurog with postscript concerning Neil's Native American friend Roy Tyner (Neil Castles Family Collection).

Buddy Baker, Cale Yarborough, Dick Hutcherson, Tiny Lund, G.C. Spencer, and Roy Mayne. Very strange indeed.

Speaking of Speedway, it is interesting to note that MGM filmed the movie twice, with the Presley/Sinatra 1968 version the latter. In 1929, two of the most popular male and female actors headlined the top-notch comedy/drama that was made as a silent film two years after talkies had arrived. It starred William Haines, who at the time was the number-one box office draw, as race driver Bill Whipple. His co-star was the beautiful Anita Page, who played Pat Bonner, and was second in popularity in 1929 only to Greta Garbo. Calling the shots

Lobby card for MGM's 1929 version of *Speedway* starring William Haines and Anita Page, directed by 1930 Academy Award nominee Harry Beaumont (Internet).

Five. Elvis Is in the Building

for Speedway *was Harry Beaumont, nominated that year as Best Director for* The Broadway Melody, *also starring Page. Surprisingly,* The Broadway Melody *was the first talkie to win the Best Picture Academy Award and was released on June 6, 1929.* Speedway *was a silent and was released on September 9, 1929, over three months later. Why* Speedway *was not a talking picture has likely been lost to the passage of time. However, MGM sent several camera crews to the 1929 Indianapolis 500 to capture actual footage used in* Speedway. *The racing scenes are very exciting, including several actual crashes, one of which claimed the life of racer Bill Spence. As in the 1968 version, there were race drivers credited with their work on the movie, including Harry Hartz as a driver and Leon Duray and Deacon Litz performing stunts just as Neil Castles did uncredited in the 1967 World 600. MGM filmed* Speedway *twice, 29 years apart, and both are worthy examples of auto racing cinema.*

As the 1960s drew to a close, the challenge of a long and incredibly fast superspeedway loomed on the horizon. And to deal with it, the slickest, most streamlined stock car to ever appear in NASCAR was introduced. The 1970s would find Neil Castles more involved than ever in racing and Hollywood.

Six

Inspections, Rescues, Wings and Protests

Every race involves one of the necessary evils of auto racing: inspections. It seems the independents were often singled out as a group in what could often be called harassment. The inspectors were frequently the source great angst. Some things the inspectors did were unreasonable. However, Neil was like all the others: looking for an edge. One inspector in particular was a pill.

Bill Gazaway wasn't too hard to get along with. His brother Joe was a pain in the ass from day one. Before the Gazaways was Norris Friel. He was a trip. He ran NASCAR just like he wanted to. He didn't allow women in the pits. He wouldn't allow any women inside the racetrack if he could keep them out. He wanted to keep out Buck's wife, my wife, and everybody else's wife out. He would allow them to go to the scorers' stand only because Joe Epton wanted it, but they couldn't go to the concession stand or nothing else. He couldn't tell Epton what to do. So I made it a point to park my car right under the scorers' stand everywhere that we went. My children could stay in the car, Jean could score the race and look down at them, and we could be sure that all the kids were took care of. All the wives were sitting there together.

Some of the places you could maybe find an edge was in the body, the chassis, and the fueling system.

One of the main things were the spoilers. You had to have the spoiler exactly the right height. If it was too high or too low you had to change it. All the templates had to fit the cars. Anywhere we went you had to pull one cylinder head and let them check the bore and stroke. They also had to check the cam to see if it was the stock cam for that engine. There was a little bit of hanky-panky that went on with that situation. Willie Thompson had an old lathe he carried with him and put a dial indicator on each lobe and turned

Six. Inspections, Rescues, Wings and Protests

it to be sure all the lobes were correct. Me and the inspectors had a pretty good understanding. I'm doing my thing, you're doing yours. If you want me to change something I'll do it over the week. I ain't doing it at the racetrack. The biggest place to get an advantage was on the chassis. Everybody was trying to cheat just a little bit to get it a little lower here and a little higher there. At one time the Dodges had a screw jack in the floor and you could adjust the torsion bars. You take a ratchet and put it down under the seat, then slide it out and adjust the torsion bar during the race. You could either make it loose or tight.

I had a rear-end cooler and a transmission cooler that sat right behind the seat. Well, one of them really was a rear-end cooler and the other one was supposed to be a transmission cooler, but that was spare gas to get you down pit road if you ran out. I had a pump on top to pump the rear-end grease. The only thing was that if you flipped the switch it pumped into the gas tank. I've still got it over in the trailer.

All them damn Ford cars from Holman and Moody inside that roll bar padding on the left side had a switch you could switch over to auxiliary fuel. I don't know who it was coming down pit road, but the car in front of me was out of gas coasting and a stream of gas came flying out of the overflow 'cause he flipped the switch the wrong way. There were several Chevrolets that was built that had two fire walls about a foot apart and inside those two fire walls was a five-gallon tank full of fuel. But don't wreck or you'll get burned up.

They once disqualified Smokey Yunick's Chevelle when they had the gas tank off of it checking it. He got aggravated with them, cranked it up, and drove it all the way back to the shop on the river. It didn't even have a gas tank on it. And if you bought a racecar from another team, don't drill any holes in it until you find out what you're drilling. There was no telling what you might drill into.

Those carburetors with the restrictor plates were sealed up by NASCAR Inspectors and there was no way to trick those up, right? Could you?

NASCAR put them plates under your carburetor and screwed the nuts on the studs and they put a seal on it. Like when you go through inspection they just checked that seal to make sure you didn't take the carburetor off and do nothing to it. It was just four studs sticking in the manifold that held the carburetor on. Well, you could screw them studs out. And take the threads off of them and drill right through the stud and put a little teeny fine Allen set screw and thread it through that hole you drilled into the bottom stud. You could take that Allen screw and screw it back about half a turn or a turn and you could pick the stud up and pull the carburetor up off that son of a bitch and do what you wanted to and put it back on. I seen it done. I knew how it worked.

Back in those days, unlike today, the infield was literally a city often much larger than where many of the drivers and crews called home. Today the fans are segregated from the participants and their million-dollar motor homes. But in the '60s through the '80s, it was much looser and somewhat lawless.

Me and Buck Baker bought the first two Winnebagos that were ever in NASCAR. We went up to Marion, North Carolina, and bought them from Tom Johnson. We wanted to have living quarters and we were the first two. We were in the infield at Daytona and everybody had their motor homes parked out there. Jean and I and our friends Neil and Bunny Dickens from Nashville were there. We put the grill outside the motor home and Jean and Bunny were inside cutting up salad and had the table set. We put the steaks on the grill out there and it was cold and freezing. Neil and me were standing out there watching the steaks, turning them over, and went in the motor home to get us some hot coffee. We went back out to turn the steaks over and the damn grill, steaks, and all were gone. They stole the grill, steaks, and all! Them damn thieves stole our dinner *and* grill. I had to get me a pass to get out through the tunnel and we went out in Neil's Lincoln to eat and came back in.

If the infields of the 1960s were lawless and unruly, help was on the way in the name of Brother Bill. Neil was there first again and helped recruit a congregation.

At the first Talladega race, some guy came in there with an old ragged trailer. He had a little homemade church built on it with three rows of seats in it. They called him Brother Bill. He was going to have a church service before the race. Some people agreed and some didn't agree. Race morning after they had the drivers' meeting, everybody headed back towards their pit spots there. He was supposed to have morning church service. So Brother Bill came down through there and asked me, "Are you going to come to church?" I said, "Yeah, I'll come to church." I got ready to start that way and

Six. Inspections, Rescues, Wings and Protests

I caught Step, a guy that worked for me. I got him by the arm and went walking down through there going to that little church. It was only big enough for three people. I walked down through there and walked past Maurice Petty and grabbed him by the shirt and said, "Come on." "What do you want with me?" "You're going to church." "You think so?" "I know so." "You telling me I'm going?" "I just told you, let's go." Me and Step and Maurice were the first three that ever walked into that church. And that began Brother Bill Frazier's church services at the races. After Brother Bill was there, he came to another racetrack somewhere. He went from down in Darlington up to the Pettys and he kind of camped out up there for a long time. I don't know where he went from there.

Brother Bill Frazier's life is well documented, including his own book With God You're Always a Winner, *by Richard Guy. Thus went the '60s.*

Neil Castles was a veteran driver on the team of all-time great and future Hall of Famer Buck Baker. Neil ran hard and finished well. He had Grand National Point Standing finishes of eighth in 1965, ninth in 1966, eighth in 1967, and fourth in 1969 in what would turn out to be his career high. A new decade was coming and Neil had a long and diversified way to go.

Upon occasion, Neil would get wind of a do-or-die situation where an organization or individual was up against it, and the only solution was money. With him and his fellow competitors springing into action, help was immediately on the way. There are several examples of an impromptu rescue.

Up there at Asheville one night it was announced on the P.A. system that they had a child, a baby, that had to be flown to New York to a hospital immediately to save his life. So I grabbed up James Hylton and everybody I could get and we went through the grandstand collecting helmets full of money and pouring them out down there in a box in the pits. All through the grandstands, the infield, anything you got, throw it in here, we need it. The promoter had somebody standing by with an airplane if we could come up with what it would take. They flew that kid to New York before we ever started the race.

Another mission of mercy took a lot more planning with the same results.

I was in the office at the Charlotte Motor Speedway talking to the president, Richard Howard. There was a writer in there doing a story about the

Holy Angels Nursery in Mount Holly/Belmont, North Carolina. They had gone broke and the children were getting no care, no nothing. They were discussing what they could do to promote some money for that Holy Angels Nursery. Richard looked at me and said, "What do you think we can do?"

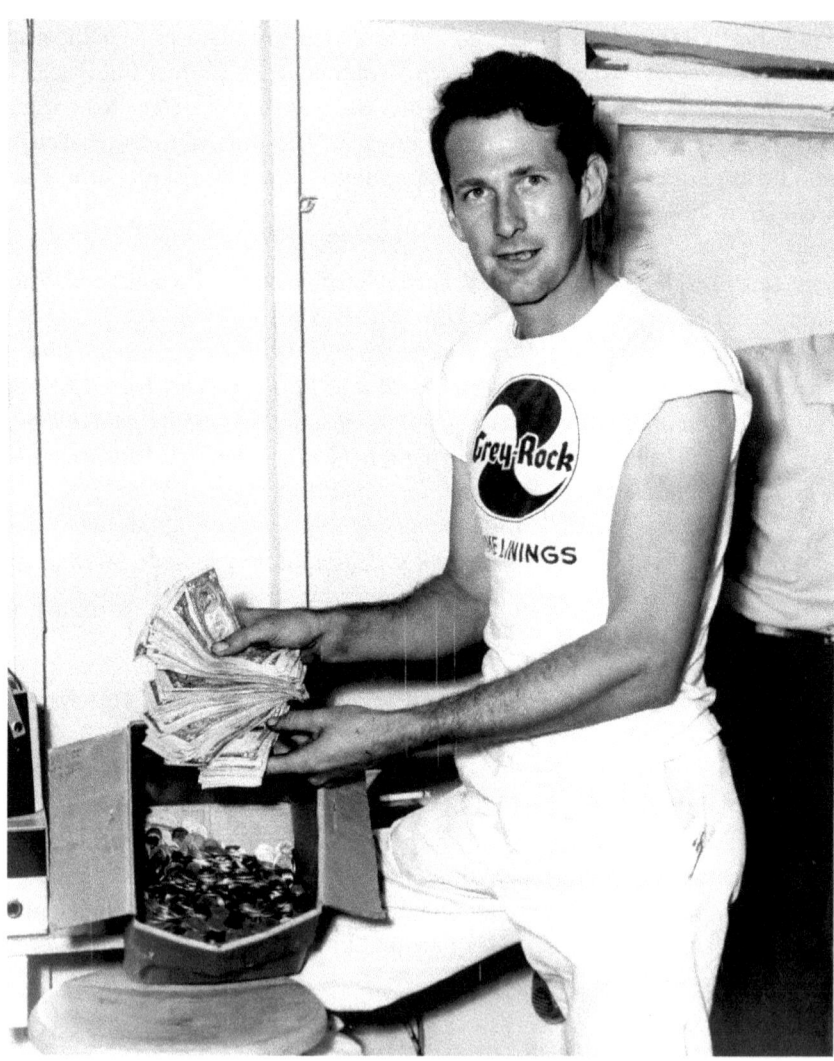

Neil Castles fans out the bills with a box of coins he, James Hylton, and others collected from fans in Asheville to fly a sick child to New York for an operation in about 1967 (Neil Castles Family Collection).

Six. Inspections, Rescues, Wings and Protests

"The best thing we can do is have an open house at the speedway for the Holy Angels Nursery right before the race. Have a one-day open house. I'll take that old car that's about worn out and we'll fix it where somebody can ride in it. We'll take a 55-gallon barrel and anybody that can put some money in it that don't rattle, folding money, I'll ride everybody that's there all day long as long as they're putting money in the barrel." We put two 55-gallon barrels out on the racetrack and made an open house day for the nursery.

In the meantime, Roy Tyner had blown the engine in that old Pontiac of his, and he was in Richard's office wanting to get some help to put an engine in it. Richard said, "Go do whatever you have to do to get the thing fixed." So I went to Carolina Machine Shop over there and told them, "Roy's going to bring some stuff in here. Fix whatever he needs so he can put it together." He was going to bring his car back after it was fixed to ride people around to help get his car running. Well, he never did get the damn thing running in time, and I ended up with the machine shop bill. I don't know what-all Roy got into later on, but Roy Tyner was born with a silver spoon in his mouth.

We saved the Holy Angels Nursery. They had a little nun that didn't weigh 50 pounds soaking wet. Her name was Sister Teresa. In the morning when we put those barrels out there on the racetrack, I picked her up and put her in the car. We rode around the racetrack real sensible two or three times and I picked her out of that car like a toy doll. From then on I went and talked to her several times.

I don't how much money we got, but we wore that old Dodge out all day. Fact of the matter, I had Pete Taylor take that old engine out and trash it. It was burnt slam up. All it was was start and go, start and go. And that was one of those hemi engines from up at Nichels.

So Neil not only orchestrated saving the Holy Angels Nursery, but bailed out Roy Tyner's racing operation at the same time.

It appeared that Neil had received a big break when he landed a seat in Ray Fox's top-notch Dodge Charger number 3. Neil and Ray went back a decade and a half to the days of chunking under-performing Fish Carburetors in the Halifax River in Daytona. But all was not as it appeared.

Fox had been in a bind with Chrysler. He was very mad because Chrysler told him to put me in the car instead of somebody he wanted. Fox had a thing where he thought he was a little better than anybody else. Me and Goldsmith went to Darlington together and practiced before the race. Fox did everything in the world that he could to screw it up. From the time we qualified and put the car in the garage area until race day, when they dropped that green flag, you had to put both feet on the dash to turn the steering wheel. Fox had screwed the whole front end up. I run it for a long time and I give out. I was getting ready to come down pit road and tell him to put Pearson in it because he was out of the race. Well, he couldn't have drove it either. At Charlotte, somebody and me got in the grass on the front straightaway and in that grass I got turned backwards and I went into the wall in one. I backed it in the wall. I was glad that son of a bitch hit the wall because I was so tired I couldn't get out.

The two races Neil ran for Ray Fox were mostly quite forgettable. At Darlington in the 1969 Rebel 400 on May 10, he started 11th and blew an engine for 29th. In the 600 at Charlotte on May 25, Neil started 12th and crashed as he described for 28th.

As the summer was fading, NASCAR opened on September 14, 1969, the super-fast Alabama International Motor Speedway at Talladega, and all was not well. The tires were blistering after only a few laps, maybe ten at the most. Bill France was adamant the Talladega 500 would be held as scheduled. So Richard Petty formed the PDA, the Professional Drivers Association, and most of the top drivers followed suit and refused to race. Bill France even got in a car and turned some laps, then enlisted the help of pony cars from the support Grand American Series race the day before to fill out the field.

Tires. The biggest issue was tires. The racetrack didn't bother me. It wasn't the speed. You were more or less used to that, day in day out. I agreed that I would not run the race. We all agreed that we'd either run the race or we wouldn't. I stood right there in the middle of it and agreed I'd stay with them. I told Richard Howard to put whoever you want to in the car because I'm not going to race. I said I wouldn't and I didn't. It came time to start the race and Richard said, "We're going to put somebody in that car and let it run a little bit and park it." He put Les Snow in the car and I stuck by what I said. I wouldn't do it. I was right there. As soon as Snow pulled the car in, I loaded it on my truck and I brought it home with me. I don't think Richard Brickhouse won the race, but they said he did.

Sticking to his word, as did most of the top drivers, Neil sat this one out in protest. His car with Les Snow aboard turned two laps and retired for 33rd.

Six. Inspections, Rescues, Wings and Protests

Meanwhile, Richard Brickhouse scored his one and only Grand National win subbing for Paul Goldsmith, edging out Jim Vandiver. Jim led most of the race in the seat Ray Fox had turned over to Bobby Johns after Neil left it. Johns would not drive it either, sticking with the PDA. It was a black eye for NASCAR, but Neil Castles stuck to his guns and took the day off.

The advent of the superspeedway at Talladega brought about a new emphasis on aerodynamics. Chrysler had made their fleet of racecars for 1969 undoubtedly the slickest stock car racing will ever see, and their drivers were known as Winged Warriors. Neil "Soapy" Castles was perfect for the name.

In 1970, Chrysler furnished us with a kit to put on the cars we had. We had to take our Charger 500s and put the winged car kits onto them. We had the blueprints and everybody put them on the same. I think I had three. We had to drill through the back, mount two things in the floor for it to set to, and put pins in it.

At Riverside I tore the car all to pieces. I was following Bobby Allison, I think, where you go up that hill and make that hard right turn by the grand-

In February of 1970, Neil Castles was one of Chrysler Corporation's "Winged Warriors" with his sleek Dodge Daytona seen during "Speed Weeks" at the Daytona International Speedway (Neil Castles Family Collection).

stand and an engine blew right in front of me. I hit that oil and I hit that outside wall on the driver's side and it dazed me. The worst thing I remember about it was when I came to my senses, this guy was on the other side of the wall with a fire extinguisher stuck inside the car through the window. I told him, "Don't do that! Don't you do that!" As soon as I cranked it and got it running I took off. They said the wing off my car went over that grandstand like a helicopter blade. It left. After that, we had to drill them and put steel cables through them. We put a steel cable up through the wing and it came down and hooked in the floor so no matter what you tore up, it would stay in place. Anyway, I got it going again and came in the pits and they cut part of the door off and the left front fender. Then, coming down that long backstretch under the bridge, I come off in there with somebody and we both spun and I hit the wall on the other side. I come back in the pits and they took the right front fender off and the right door. Then I got in another crash somewhere that same day. When I come in the pits after the race was over, there wasn't much left but part of a chassis. I was kind of aggravated and sat on a bench looking at what I had left to take home. Ronnie Householder [head of Chrysler Racing Division] came by and said, "I believe you're going to need a little more sheet metal. I have never seen anything torn up that bad and stay running long enough to finish the race."

The record shows that on January 18, 1970, Neil started the Motor Trend 500 in 18th place and soldiered home a very respectable seventh, 15 laps behind winner A.J. Foyt and just two behind the undisputed Riverside master Dan Gurney. Neil proved himself right off the bat to be a true Winged Warrior. But wait, there is more.

We had picked up these new Dodge trucks at Baker Equipment Company. Goldsmith got one and I got one. Householder told me, "I tell you what I want you to do. Load that car on that new truck and take it to Ray Nichels in Highland, Indiana." So I did and they unloaded my old car up there and loaded a test car that needed to go to Charlotte to be tested. That car that I brought back was that old green car number 88 that nobody wanted. Nobody wanted that damn car because it was green. They loaded gears, transmissions, and two engines in that box behind us. They loaded it down. At that time, Chrysler had half of the Goodyear Building at the Charlotte Speedway. Me and Paul Goldsmith took turns hauling the dirt. I'd drive the dump truck for half the day and load it to grade that land up there on the hill to put up that

Six. Inspections, Rescues, Wings and Protests

Goodyear Building. Goldsmith and them had half of it for the Chrysler cars. They sent my car back to Charlotte to Goldsmith's up there. They put new sheet metal on it and fixed it. The Dodge Daytona was a lot more stable than the Charger 500 'cause we could change the spoilers, lower the front end, and it was closer to the ground with less air under the car. It was more stable that way.

Neil recorded some fine finishes in 1970 with or without a wing, such as thirds at Hampton, Virginia; Maryville and Nashville, Tennessee; fourths at Columbia, South Carolina; Beltsville, Maryland; and Malta, New York; fifths at Richmond, Virginia; Thompson, Connecticut; and Columbia; ninth at Talladega, Alabama; and a historic second place on September 30, 1970, at the North Carolina State Fairgrounds.

That was a nice racetrack in Raleigh. It was an easy race to run and I felt comfortable doing it. We just knew it was a dirt track race, but not the *last* Grand National dirt track race ever. Petty was driving Jabe Thomas' car. Jabe Thomas was just a good old guy and had a pretty good car. Between him and Elmo they were always pulling tricks on people. Petty didn't want to put his good car on that dirt track because they had to have it for whatever the next race was. They took Jabe's car to Petty's and fixed it and painted it. John Sears was on the pole, Petty won it, and I was second.

We had a $500 deal to come Raleigh when we signed the entry blank. That was a $500 deal, supposedly. After the race, we were hunting the promoter and he was gone. He was definitely gone. I don't remember his name, but there was a boy that was with him that had the pace car. And later on the pace car was sitting out in the middle of the racetrack with nobody around it. Everybody was waiting on their deal money. So somebody sent word to the hotel that they didn't like things the way it was and there was going to be a big change if he didn't get back down there with the deal money. Well, he came back with the deal money and some people kind of confronted him. He went around and give everybody their $500. Wendell come over there with us and said, "Neil, you know that man done give me $500 and give all my boys $500. What did y'all do to him?" "We leaned on him a little bit."

When they loaded up and creaked out of the North Carolina State Fairgrounds that fall Wednesday night, the curtain sadly fell on the Grand National dirt track era. What is even sadder was that no one there even knew it.

Neil remembers a real winged car oddity.

Neil "Soapy" Castles

There was only one winged car that started a short-track race and that was at Ona, West Virginia. Buddy Baker was driving for Cotton, and Cotton didn't take a car for Baker to race. Well, Baker was there and they had advertised him running the race and all. They come down there and made me a deal to let him start my winged car, and he started my winged car in that race. It's the only time a winged car ever started a short-track race. I ran the whole race. At that time I had two numbers, 06 and 86. I could put a piece of red tape across there and make an 8 out of the 0. Buddy didn't have number 86, I did. Buck borrowed it from me to get Buddy started. You look back and my old convertible was 86. When Shuman wasn't any longer using 86, I took that number and put it on the convertible. He gave it to me. If anybody had a number that somebody else wanted, you had to sign it over to them.

The record shows that on Tuesday, August 11, 1970, at International Raceway Park, in Ona, West Virginia, Neil started fifth and finished third behind Richard Petty and James Hylton in the West Virginia 300. As for Buddy Baker, he scorched Neil's winged Dodge Daytona number 86 around the .437-mile paved speedway with the fourth fastest speed of the night. That fulfilled Buddy's and the promoter's obligation to compete because number 86 retired after seven laps due to "Brakes." Neil assuredly told Buddy to come into the pits and put on the brakes and get out after a few laps. The 21st-place finish was worth $225 of purse money plus whatever Neil was paid to let Baker hitch a ride for the night. And why would Neil even carry a Dodge Daytona to Ona in the first place? The Yankee 400 was the next race five days later on Sunday, August 16, 1970, at Michigan International Speedway in Brooklyn, Michigan, where Neil took off the tape, made it number 06 again, and brought it home 12th.

With the end of the Grand National season in 1970, Neil Castles completed a string of points finishes beginning in 1965 of eighth, ninth, eighth, twelfth, fourth, and fifth. He was competitive every time out with his best yet to come.

For 1971, the wings were gone, except for Dick Brooks' one shot with a small block in the Daytona 500, and the Winston Cup arrived. The season consisted of a whopping 48 races, but new series sponsor R.J. Reynolds Tobacco Company would gut the schedule of its short-track and mid-week events the next year. Neil opened up with three top tens in his first seven races. Race number eight for Neil was the debut of the newly paved historic half-mile in Columbia, South Carolina. Well over 30 cars showed up for 22 spots to usher in the blacktop and Neil's Dodge Charger 500 did not sport a sponsor. He was making a protest statement: "Free Lt. Calley."

Six. Inspections, Rescues, Wings and Protests

In his protest statement, Neil Castles supported convicted U.S. Army Lt. William Calley on his Dodge Charger 500 at Columbia Speedway, finishing ninth on April 8, 1971 (Perry Allen Wood Racing Archives).

Everybody was in a big fuss on the TV all hollering about Lt. Calley this, that, and the other. So I said, "What in the hell is the use to mess with him? He ain't done nothing." But they were putting him in jail anyway. I put that on both rear quarter panels and that created a lot of smoke. It was my damn car and I'll do what I want to with it. That was just like I did a movie called *Hot Summer in Barefoot County*. I did the whole quarter panels *Hot Summer in Barefoot County* on my car. That was a movie where this guy wrote a script because his daddy owned a drive-in theater. He worked there and wanted to write a movie. There were no stars in it. But I run "Free Lt. Calley" on my car because I wanted to, no matter whether anybody else liked it or not.

From Wikipedia: "William Laws Calley Jr., is a former United States Army officer convicted by court-martial of murdering 22 unarmed South Vietnamese civilians in the My Lai Massacre on March 16, 1968, during the Vietnam War. While not technically exonerated, after three and a half years of house arrest, Calley was released pursuant to a ruling by federal judge J. Robert Elliott, who

Neil "Soapy" Castles

found that Calley's trial had been prejudiced by pre-trial publicity, denial of subpoenas of certain defense witnesses, refusal of the United States House of Representatives to release testimony taken in executive session of its My Lai investigation, and inadequate notice of the charges. His initial conviction faced widespread public opposition both due to the campaign circumstances of civilian embedded Viet Cong, and due to Calley being singled out as the sole officer convicted with respect to the massacre."

Neil Castles was far from alone in his speaking out for Lt. Calley. Wikipedia goes on to state: "Georgia's Governor Jimmy Carter instituted American Fighting Man's Day and asked Georgians to drive for a week with their lights on. Indiana's governor asked all state flags to be flown at half-staff for Calley, and Utah's and Mississippi's governors also disagreed with the verdict. The Arkansas, Kansas, Texas, New Jersey, and South Carolina legislatures requested clemency for Calley. Alabama's Governor George Wallace visited Calley in the stockade and requested that President Richard Nixon pardon him. After the conviction, the White House received over 5,000 telegrams; the ratio was 100 to 1 in favor of leniency. In a telephone survey of the American public, 79 percent disagreed with the verdict, 81 percent believed that the life sentence Calley had received was too stern, and 69 percent believed Calley had been made a scapegoat."

Not alone in his feelings, on Thursday, April 8, 1971, one week after Lt. Calley's conviction, with "Free Lt. Calley" emblazoned in red on both rear quarter panels of his white number 06, Neil qualified seventh and finished ninth. Everyone at Columbia Speedway knew just exactly how Neil Castles felt. They always did. Never one to follow others or help maintain the status quo, Neil developed his own look partially out of necessity.

Back then, I was the only one racing that wore cowboy boots and a black hat. The reason I wore them boots was because my feet are bad. I didn't have any arch support. I could walk all day with those boots on, but if I had to walk with other shoes on I couldn't go across the street. That's the reason I started wearing cowboy boots was because of my feet. The black hat you can figure out for yourself.

It was not because he was a bad guy. Neil was anything but. However, if one was looking for a scrap, Neil could oblige as well as anybody.

A half dozen races after Columbia, Neil was in Talladega for the Winston 500 on May 16, 1971.

Six. Inspections, Rescues, Wings and Protests

I took all my winged Dodge Daytonas and converted them back to Charger 500s, a short-track car and a superspeedway car. I took two of them to Talladega. Gazaway came to me and said, "I got a man that wants to buy two racecars today. He'll pay cash for them. What would you take for those two Dodges?" I said, "Well, I don't know. I hadn't planned on selling them. That's all I've got left is them two Dodges." He said, "Come up with a figure and let me know in a few minutes." I thought about it and sold them two cars and brought them back home to Charlotte on my truck. I was give out and spent the night. I took the cars to this guy up in Greensboro and unloaded them to come home. Then I took what I got out of the two cars and went to Cotton and bought another one.

Frequently donning a black hat, Neil Castles was not one to be trifled with and wore this subtle reminder to those who were unsure (Neil Castles Family Collection).

A newcomer sprang onto the scene in 1971, and a few races into the season, Neil decided to give him a hand before somebody got hurt.

Walter Ballard showed up in Atlanta with a racecar and we went out to practice. I followed that fool and thought, "Hell, he's going to bounce that son of a bitch off the wall before he ever gets around the racetrack. I felt sorry for him. Hell, he'd go in the corner on the bottom of the racetrack and he'd be up rubbing the wall and come back down and couldn't get straight. He come back in the garage area and I was parked over there and he was across from me. I walked over there and I said, "You don't know me, but I'll tell you what. You can't drive that damn car because you've got a problem." He said, "What's that?" I said, "You ain't got no spoiler on the deck lid and it's sliding right out from under your ass." He said, "It is, isn't it?" We went over to my truck and got a piece of sheet metal down and put it on the work bench. I bent it and formed it and went over and put it on the back of that car. He run the whole race with it. It was the first time he ever had a car that he could drive. That's where I got tied up with Walter Ballard. He's got a shop over on Statesville Avenue now.

Yet another example of Neil Castles dropping everything to assist someone in need who did not even know to ask for it. That may have been Walter Ballard's lucky day.

With ten top tens and 22nd in the 1971 Winston Cup Point Standings, Neil was about to get news that would send him to new heights as a racecar driver when NASCAR made another groundbreaking announcement: "NASCAR's new Grand National East Division for late model stock cars will begin its 1972 season with the Bold City 200 at the Jacksonville Speedway in Jacksonville, Florida, March 14. The division, which will have more than 20 races this year, blends the Grand National stock car of the last four model years with the lighter and quick Grand American cars." It was a gift from the racing gods, and Neil Castles was ready to cash in.

Seven

That Championship Feeling

NASCAR's second Winston Cup campaign in 1972 was mostly a struggle for Neil, with one top ten at Rockingham, a tenth, and a dismal 30th in the standings in 21 starts. However, Neil ran hard and tough in the new Grand National East Division and became the man to beat.

I run both series. I run every race I could run. I won two races in Greenville, South Carolina, and Maryville, Tennessee. I left Greenville and went straight to Nashville. Our daughter Donna and David Pearson's kids were out there in the infield playing ball with all them old trailers parked there and she fell over a trailer tongue and broke her arm. So I left there and went to Nashville.

At Nashville, a hole come in the racetrack about halfway through the race. You had to either go above it, or come below it, or just knock the front end out from under the car if you hit it. Tiny Lund blew the engine in his car during the race. He was in a Camaro that somebody from Spartanburg owned. When the race was over with, we come in the pits and the damn rod had come right through the pan on Tiny's car. They had another engine, but they didn't have another oil pan. So I sat down there, me and Neil Dickens on the back of my truck, and took two hammers and dollied that hole in that oil pan together. I took an acetylene torch and welded that hole in that pan. It was two o'clock in the morning when I left there after fixing that oil pan for him.

I run wide open like an idiot to get to Maryville, Tennessee, and I was the first one at the gate. I couldn't get in because there was nobody there. Somehow the lock broke on the gate and I got in. I jacked the car up and set it on stands and had to change two torsion bars, two rear springs, and a gear. From Nashville to there, I had to change the chassis and the gear.

After I won the race I was sitting on a box in the infield and I was looking

Neil "Soapy" Castles

for the promoter. I wanted my $500 deal money. I didn't sign an entry blank unless I was going to get my money. The promoter told Gazaway, "I'm not paying him no damn $500 deal money. Did you see that trophy I gave him?" I said, "Yeah, and it's down there in the truck." I told Gazaway, "Go down there to the truck and get that trophy. I'm going to feed it to this son of a bitch." Gazaway told the promoter, "I think you better pay him." And he did. I give him his little trophy and he took it home with him.

According to the records, on May 14, 1972, at Smoky Mountain Raceway in Maryville, Tennessee, Neil Castles started second beside pole-sitter Dave Marcis and a race-long battle ensued. Marcis had led for 156 of the 200 laps when his engine blew with 17 to go, and Neil rumbled beneath the checkers just ahead of H.B. Bailey. Soapy was cleaning up and became the man to beat as the inaugural Grand National East season headed into summer.

And a hot summer of '72 it was, and tempers were short enough without having somebody to stir the pot. An unfortunate incident in the garage area of the Atlanta International Raceway on July 22 posed a threat to Neil Castles' point-leading run. The ramifications were enormous.

We went to a dinner in Atlanta and all of the drivers were invited. Russ DeVault was a reporter for the Winston-Salem newspaper and was there asking us questions about one thing and another. The next morning he showed up at the racetrack in the garage area with a handful of documents from the State of North Carolina. He had gone to Raleigh and got the driving records of everybody in NASCAR and was going to write a book or a story about how dangerous it was for the NASCAR drivers to be on the highways in the State of North Carolina. He had me and Buck Baker named right up front on this big stack of documents. He said, "You believe this, don't you?" And I said, "No, I don't. That's bullshit! You're fishing for something that ain't worth a damn to nobody except to hurt somebody's feelings." So I tore them all in half. All the stuff he had from Raleigh I tore in half and threw in the garbage can. He turned around and jumped at me and said, "You can't do that," and I smacked him and he slid right under the edge of somebody's racecar. I popped him upside the head and he slid across the floor.

Well, everybody in the garage area was glad to see that damn handful of records gone. He had one on Richard Petty that was a two-page document. He had how many people had a speeding ticket, how many people got caught driving drunk, how many people had been arrested in the State of North Car-

Seven. That Championship Feeling

olina driving with suspensions and shit, everybody in the damn garage area was pissed at him and would've liked to killed him. I turned around to Baker and said, "Buck, you want this shit advertised about you?" Buck had looked at it and said, "Hell, No!" That ended it.

Not quite. The damage was done. The fallout was on the way.

DeVault went back to Winston-Salem and started a big deal with NASCAR, and NASCAR wanted to throw me out for assaulting a newspaper reporter. NASCAR was going to suspend me for life. We had a meeting and finally a bunch of drivers got together and said, "You going to suspend all of us? Every one of us were named in it." Bill France said, "No, I'm not going to suspend anybody but Neil. Neil's the one who smacked him." In the meantime I think they fined me $1,000 or $100 [actually $250] and were throwing me out of NASCAR.

We met with NASCAR again and I wouldn't agree to nothing and I didn't intend to. That's when NASCAR jumped me big-time and said I couldn't come back to any racetracks at all. I was done for. I said, "I'll tell you what. I'm going up there and find that son of a bitch and if he wants something to bitch about I'll give him something to bitch about. I'll knock his damn brains

PENALTY NOTICE

TO: Bill Gazaway, John Bruner, Sr., Lin Kuchler
NAME: Neil Castles   DATE: July 22, 1972 (OF RULES INFRACTION)
Address: 6525 Sullins Road, Charlotte, North Carolina 28214
NASCAR No.: GND-06   RECEIVED AT NASCAR: July 24, 1972
RULES INFRACTION: Fighting in garage area.
REPORTED BY: NASCAR Official
TRACK: Atlanta International Raceway
PENALTY: $250 fine
DISPOSITION:
DATE: July 25, 1972

PN - 1,000—10/25/71—H

Documentation that NASCAR was not going to take slugging reporters lightly. Neil never paid a cent and gave the bruised newsman a classic apology (Neil Castles Family Collection).

out." France said, "Now, wait a minute. Let's smooth this thing out." They calmed it down and I didn't get fined nothing. I had to go to a mediation with all the press and they wanted me to apologize to DeVault. And I did. I said, "You're the first son of a bitch I've ever apologized to and I'm glad we're here."

A story written by renowned motorsports journalist Bob Myers reported in the February 1973 edition of Southern Automotive Journal *that Joe Hawkins, the promoter of the upcoming race at Winston-Salem's Bowman Gray Stadium, had refused Neil's entry until he apologized to DeVault. Since he was nursing a six-point lead over Elmo Langley at the time, missing the Winston-Salem race would have torpedoed Neil's championship chances, so he apologized. Neil obviously remembers it the way it was told here. From then on, Neil "Soapy" Castles held Elmo Langley at bay and captured the title.*

They declared me the champion of 1972. When we went to Daytona in February of 1973 they gave me a championship ring, a plaque, and a trophy. Tiny was driving that damn Ford of Elmo's and he was sure he was going to outrun me with that Ford for the points. I outrun him and that's what determined that he did not win the damn championship. I did.

NASCAR's 1973 Victory Dinner

Clipping from an unidentified publication showing NASCAR's 1972 stock car champions Richard Petty (at right in left photograph) in Winston Cup and Neil Castles (second from left in right photograph) in Grand National East receiving their trophies from Bernie Stewart (Neil Castles Family Collection).

Seven. That Championship Feeling

Jean and Neil Castles at the NASCAR Awards Ceremony in Daytona Beach, Florida, sometime in the 1970s. Not 1973, as Neil's attire does not match the previous photograph (Neil Castles Family Collection).

Neil "Soapy" Castles

In his first win at Greenville, South Carolina, on Saturday, April 1, 1972, Neil outran Elmo Langley and David Pearson, who were on the lead lap with LeeRoy Yarbrough one behind in fourth and Charlie Blanton fifth back. At Maryville, Tennessee, Neil started second and took his second win of the year. Neil Castles in his Howard Furniture Dodge started 14 of the 15 races with two wins, ten top fives, 13 top tens, and the inaugural Grand National East Division Championship. He won it by a whopping seven and a half points over Elmo Langley and won $19,730 in purses, which does not count his ever-present deal money. Neil had come a long way from when Dippo Kelly towed his Soap Box Derby car with an old A Model Ford to winning a champion's rewards in Daytona Beach. Buddy Shuman named Neil "Soapy" for that boyhood episode, and was no doubt looking down and smiling big that day.

It was not only Neil's championship, but it was his sponsor Richard Howard's, too. Neil explains that his sponsor was quite a man.

He was strictly a promoter, strictly business. At one time I didn't have a racecar at all. I was trying to figure where I was going to get a car, and so I went and sat down and talked to Richard about it. He had a furniture store in Denver, North Carolina. He was involved with a lot of things. He built steakhouses. He came out with a thing called Biscuitville that were all over the country. He was also involved with Wray Frazier Camper Sales. He owned that cross-country campground at Denver for years and he also owned Denver Equipment Company. Denver Equipment Company sold all the dishes, silverware, china, and stuff to them steakhouses he owned. It was up there on 150 in Mooresville near Howard's Furniture. He helped a lot of people. He and Bobby Isaac were pretty close. If you see where Bobby Isaac drove my car like at the race at Rockingham, that was when I was doing a movie in Wilmington and that's what Richard wanted to do. He was very helpful with the Holy Angels Nursery. He's passed away now.

A few years earlier, Richard Howard had come to the rescue again on a huge scale.

They repossessed the Atlanta racetrack. There was a big fight about it and Joe Littlejohn was in on it. Finally to settle the damn thing, I went to Richard and he give me the money to pay it off. I went straight to Atlanta and paid the damn thing off. He and L.G. DeWitt from Rockingham came up with the money and they were the ones that saved the racetrack in Atlanta.

Seven. That Championship Feeling

I was the gofer that delivered the money. When there were things like that going on he wanted done, he'd just call me and say, "I want you to go do so and so."

Obviously Richard Howard was a man of means, a forward thinker, and his ideas usually came to be. Such was the racecar he wanted to build in the spring of 1971 for the World 600.

He wanted to build a brand new Chevrolet to run Charlotte. He took me to Bank of America and I borrowed the money to build the car and he guaranteed the loan. I borrowed the money and Richard signed the note. He took that money and give it to Junior Johnson to build that car. The deal was when the race was over, I get the car. They were going to have the best Chevrolet to run at Charlotte.

They had a big to-do about who was going to drive the car. Richard said, "I don't care who drives it. I want it on the pole." I said, "If that's the case and you've got me in the middle of this damn thing, I'm going to put Charlie Glotzbach in it. He can qualify faster than any bastard you got on the racetrack." Richard said, "Do you think he's that good at qualifying?" I told him, "Put him in it and see where he ends up." So we put Glotzbach in the car. Nobody ever knew it, but that was my doings. So Glotzbach sat on the pole and led the whole race.

Right at the end a bunch of drunks in the grandstand filled the racetrack full of bottles. He ran over a beer bottle, busted a right front tire, and hit the wall with it leading the race with a few laps to go. I went down to the garage area and loaded it on my truck and took it home. That was my car. I was to keep it.

By breakfast the next morning, Neil got a visitor and a directive. Neil never hesitated.

I had it setting in there in my garage on jack stands and the next morning Herb Nab showed up at the shop. Herb worked for Junior. "Junior said for me to come down here and get this car ready to go. Bill France wants that car at Daytona now." We fixed it right there in the shop. Done all the front end work on it and everything. Loaded it up and I took it to Daytona. Junior's got that car and two more. In practice and qualifying we blew the engine. So Junior yanked that engine out and sent it to Wilkesboro and stuck a new engine in it. We run it in the race and blew another engine. When the race was over, I had a racecar with a blown engine.

I loaded it up and brought it home. I was still on the hook for the money with the bank. Then NASCAR wants that car at the next race after Daytona. They wanted that fast Chevrolet. Well, I went to work on a movie and Richard came down and got the car, sold it, and paid off the bank note. That was the end of it. They told me Allison picked up the car and took it. Richard or Junior sold it to someone in California. I don't know where it went. I was supposed to have kept the car for doing all that shit. I was glad to be rid of it. They'd done tore the car up, blowed all the engines, and I had a racecar with no engine in it and owed the bank $10,000.

The record shows that in the World 600, Chargin' Charlie Glotzbach sat the Howard/Castles Kmart/Pistonlube Chevrolet Monte Carlo number 3 on the pole and led frequently, crashing out with 66 laps to go for 38th. On the Fourth of July at Daytona, Glotzbach started third and the biggest explosion of the day

Some racers were asked at the last minute by Richmond Speedway promoter Paul Sawyer to go to Berlin Speedway in Marne, Michigan, for an exhibition race in the summer of 1973. Neil was glad he did as he took the checkers (Neil Castles Family Collection).

Seven. That Championship Feeling

was the Chevy's engine after only 43 laps for 37th. A week later after Neil was off the hook for the car and making movies, Charlie was really charging at Bristol, Tennessee, when he started second and led a whopping 411 of 500 laps to dominate in the Volunteer 500.

In May of 1972, Richard Howard again wanted a hot Chevrolet for the World 600 on the heels of the Charlie Glotzbach run the year before. Only this time Howard had chosen the driver himself and it was Neil's longtime competitor and friend Wendell Scott. The records show that Wendell had cut back on racing quite a bit in 1971, which showed starts in 37 of 48 of what was now Winston Cup starts for 19th in the standings. He had recorded top-ten points finishes from 1965 through 1969 and everybody involved in stock car racing knew that with a competitive ride, Wendell Scott could be a front-runner. He had raced in one other Cup Series event so far in 1972 at Martinsville with no success. Wendell was actually concentrating on the new Grand National East Series, as was Neil. Richard Howard wanted to give him that chance and told Neil to find the car. But it was not just his equipment that was lacking, and for sure it was not the color of his skin. Wendell Oliver Scott was 51 years old, and every race driver who lived long enough to crawl behind the wheel was past his prime at 50. All of them!

>The car was one of the cars that Junior Johnson had, but we didn't say that it was a top-notch car. It was a top-notch car. The car was capable of running up front all day. I don't think whatever driver you had in it would win the race, though. I think it would run in the top three all day. I got the car, I drove it myself, and to be sure it was a car that could win a race. I practiced in it at Charlotte and put Wendell in it and he practiced with it. It was a good car and Junior prepared it. Herb Nab came down and we worked on the chassis and Wendell qualified 11th. That was a reasonable qualifying time. He didn't have anything a third that good.

>At the end of the day, Wendell Scott's results were mixed. On the plus side, Wendell had not qualified that high in two years and never in his career on a superspeedway. He ran better than he ever would have in his own car around the seventh to 15th range and did it without spending one cent of his own money. The extra attention and a special post-race Curtis Turner Achievement Award presented by Turner's widow were both pluses. The downside was that the engine gave up on lap 283 just short of the three-quarter mark for a so-so 22nd place. However, on May 28, 1972, Wendell Scott finished the 600 ahead of G.C.

Spencer, Dick Brooks, Neil Castles, Donnie Allison, Can Am star Jackie Oliver, Dave Marcis, Coo Coo Marlin, David Pearson, and Bobby Isaac. The 44-year-old Wendell Scott of 1965 would have had that car a lot closer to the front.

Tiger Tom Pistone wanted to look in the car and Neil helped him get real close. He kept Tom there for a while, as Neil has about a two-foot height advantage (Neil Castles Family Collection).

The next season, 1973, it was obvious where Neil's heart was. He ran eight of 28 Winston Cup races and all 15 as defending champion of the Grand National East Division. He mustered a runner-up finish to Tiny Lund that year with three top fives and eight top tens while pocketing an embarrassing $4,785. Not embarrassing to Neil, but to NASCAR for letting him risk his life from March until November for less than he got for being Elvis' double six years earlier during a few weeks in May. Looks like MGM had a lot deeper pockets than NASCAR.

Sometime in the early '70s Neil's keen sense of awareness allowed him to once again bail out a friend when trouble was just literally just around the corner.

Seven. That Championship Feeling

We were all on pit road at Darlington getting ready to start the Southern 500 one year. Well, these people one pit down below me, I kept hearing them talk about Jim Vandiver. I thought, "Hell, what are they talking about him for? He's getting ready to start this race. I am, too." I got to looking and this guy was a damned old detective. I knew him from Charlotte. I'd seen him before. There was about four of them over there. So I just sort of eased into the edge of their conversation and listened to them. Well, Jim was in a divorce with his wife and she'd signed a bunch of warrants for him. They were going to wait until the race was over and as soon as he started to get out of the car, they were going to lock him up and take him to jail. I picked up on all that big conversation.

So I went over and got Jim by the arm and said, "Come on over here and let me tell you something. When that race is over with, you don't come down pit road. You get the hell out of that car over on that back corner, the fourth corner. That little old road goes out to the street. You get you a ride out of here." We got the checkered flag and were coming around to stop, he pulled up right there at the exit, jumped out of the car, hopped the fence, went down the hill, run out in the middle of the street, and two girls picked him up and took him to Charlotte. I didn't want it to be an embarrassing situation with all the police on him as soon as he got out of the car.

The Jim Vandiver "Escape from Darlington" yarn has been told by many for years. I was extremely fortunate to hear Jim relate an unabridged version of it at Alex Beam's Memory Lane Museum in Mooresville, North Carolina, in mid–May of 2015 as we sat side by side signing stuff. He actually got a second ride after the two ladies dropped him off halfway home. Some sport fisherman picked him up and Jim rode in the back seat the rest of the way to Charlotte with some huge smelly trophy fish. Three weeks after I was so privileged to hear that tale firsthand, Jim Vandiver escaped his earthly bonds in a Charlotte hospital after experiencing chest pains a day earlier.

Neil had countless friends in racing and one of the most colorful was another Jim named Hurtubise. Burned horribly in a crash at Milwaukee the week after the 1964 Indianapolis 500 claimed Eddie Sachs and Dave MacDonald, "Herk," as he was known, had them mold what was left of his charred fingers around a steering wheel so he could race, and he raced and won for many more years. In Declarations of Stock Car Independents, Captain America Raymond Williams calls Hurtubise "Old Crispy" due to his burns. Neil was a close friend of Jim Hurtubise and relates a flying story.

Neil "Soapy" Castles

The government had that airbase there at Daytona and owned all that land that was a swamp around the airbase. The only runway there was the one they used for the Air Force jets to get in and out on. Well, France made a deal to get the land to build the speedway, but to be able to use it you had to drain it, and that's where they dug that hole and put that lake in there. He dug dirt forever and took all that dirt out of that infield and built them turns. That dried it up enough to make the backstretch there. So you got a nice lake there directly beside the backstretch.

Well, Hurtubise flew his plane to Daytona. He filed his flight plan and was going to land on the runway at the airport, which was parallel to the backstretch at the racetrack. But Jim just slipped over a little bit and set that old seaplane down on that lake. The plane and Jim disappeared off the radar. The air traffic controllers lost him. Hell, that stirred up the whole country. Famous race driver lost in airplane crash! Hurtubise thought it was funny. He said, "Hell, I didn't have to be over there. I needed to be over here." He landed right on that lake right beside that damn runway. At the airport they thought he crashed.

One of Neil's good friends on the circuit was fellow Dodge driver and country music superstar Marty Robbins. One day, out of the blue, Marty showed his affection for Neil and another Dodge chauffeur with a very unusual gift. No bull!

Marty Robbins gave me and James Hylton registered Angus bulls. Hylton came to the house and wanted to know if we could go to Marty's and get the bulls that he give us. I didn't know anything about it until James showed up with Evelyn at the house. I hooked my horse trailer behind my Cadillac and we went to Nashville. We went to Marty's farm. They knew we were coming and I backed up to the loading chute. They loaded two Angus bulls in that trailer. That's when Hylton had a farm down there in Spartanburg, actually Inman, South Carolina. So I dropped his bull off in Inman. I brought mine home and we named it T-Bone.

T-Bone thought he was one of the horses and followed us around like a puppy. There was a golf course behind that house with an electric fence and a barbed wire fence. They'd tear the damn fence down to go in there and get golf balls. The next thing I know T-Bone was out on the golf course. So Jean went out there with a bucket of corn and that bull followed her right back to the barn. He followed us around like a puppy. Then I had to patch the fence. The golfers would take a golf club and break the wire and slide the poles out

Seven. That Championship Feeling

of the fence. Later I gave Hylton my bull. I carried it to Spartanburg and put it in the pasture with the other one.

A very strange and dangerous incident took place in the infield at Daytona on the late '60s. As with a lot of memories, time has obscured the date it happened.

When we got to Daytona they said they didn't have room for all our damn trailers in the garage area. So everybody was to take their trailers and their tow trucks that they don't have to have and put them in that lot over on the backstretch where the guardrail was between the lake and the racetrack. We weren't happy with all our stuff being stuck over there until the race was over. When the race was over with, all the guys pulled in over there to get our trailers.

When they come back with mine, I had the racecar setting there getting ready to load it. Jean and the kids were there in a brand-new Dodge Charger 500. It was brand-new when we left Charlotte with it. The guys with the trailer said that there wasn't a chain left, a tie-down left, nothing. Nobody had anything. Somebody went in there and stripped every one of those trailers. We had a pit road full of trailers and nobody had a way to tie a car down. So we started cutting up chain. You'd throw a piece of chain across the axle, put a bolt in it. Chain the rear end to the back, the front went to the front of the trailer and that's the only way we were tying them to the trailer.

Neil Castles gears up for a Winston Cup start in Bristol, Tennessee, in the 1970s (Neil Castles Family Collection).

Tom Pistone or somebody said, "There's still some of that stuff over on the backstretch if you can find it. Them people couldn't have carried it all off." I jumped in the car with Jean and the kids and we went around to the backstretch. Denny, Jean's brother was with us, and we were hunting in them weeds and stuff and we did find a few chain binders and things that didn't get carried out of there.

So we throwed them in the car and came back around the racetrack and just about the time I was going to turn onto pit road, this Mustang shot right in front of me and I nailed him in the door. Susan's face went through the windshield and she was just pouring blood. They yanked me and Jean and the kids out of the wreck, stuck us on Bill France's airplane, and flew us directly to the Charlotte Airport. They had an ambulance waiting and it took us straight to the hospital.

Stunt man Neil Castles wrecked a lot of cars on purpose. This was an accident and occurred in April 20, 1973, at Columbia Speedway in Columbia, South Carolina (Neil Castles Family Collection).

Seven. That Championship Feeling

I didn't know where that car come from. I was just running normal and wasn't in that big of a hurry. I was worrying about how we were going to tie this shit down on the trailer. They never did tell me exactly who was driving the Mustang, but it was one of the higher-ups with Ford Motor Company. The word was that he was under the influence of alcohol. They took him to a doctor and determined that he was slightly, well, he had been drinking the whole race. He was taking off out the gate. They wanted us out of town. But NASCAR didn't have no business taking our stuff and putting it way over there in that damn field where some bunch of bastards went in there hauled off everything they could steal. Hell, that's just the way it was.

The story does not end there. Get this.

I had Cotton pick that new wrecked Dodge up and bring it on up to his shop in Spartanburg. That turned out to be the short-track car I bought from Cotton and run forty-something races with it. Jean never did know that was the same car we wrecked. Cotton made a racecar out of it in a month and a half and sold it back to me. I didn't own it, Chrysler did.

Cotton Owens and Neil Castles were Dodge boys through and through and had a deep friendship and respect for each other.

In the fall of 1974, Richard Howard approached Neil again with an idea to give a racer a break and put him in a good car for one of his big races. Neil thought of only one driver that fit the bill. He was not only good, but he was a young up-and-coming local boy from a racing family that everybody knew. It turned out to be the seed of something legendary, if not sport-changing.

Well, me and Ralph Earnhardt were real good friends and I had two or three old cars at that time. Richard said, "We got to come up with some new driver for the sportsman race this year. We need something new. Let's get him a good car." Me and Ralph had talked a while back about how Dale was going to go somewhere in a few years. Before, he had been running short tracks and I run a couple of races with him. So I throwed Dale in the mix to get that ride and that's where it come from. Richard went for it immediately.

Saturday, October 5, 1974, was a cool, crisp sunny autumn afternoon and Ralph Dale Earnhardt, Sr., drove his first bigtime stock car race in Neil Castles' fast Dodge number 06. The event was the World Service Life 300, and 200 laps

Dale Earnhardt, Sr., made his first major career start in Neil's Dodge Super Bee at the Charlotte Motor Speedway on October 5, 1974, in the World Service Life 300 (Neil Castles Family Collection).

With gasoline overflowing, Neil stands in the dark shirt with the oval waiting to give Earnhardt the signal to go on October 5, 1974, in the World Service Life 300 in Charlotte (Neil Castles Family Collection).

Seven. That Championship Feeling

around the speedway's towering banks were a much, much longer distance going several times faster than Dale had ever raced before. Not only was he up to the task, he wanted more. In a race that included not only the best sportsman drivers of the day, a few of the Winston Cup regulars were on hand. Bobby Allison won it, but Dale Earnhardt started 12th and finished 13th a very respectable five laps behind and right in front of sportsman star Morgan Shepherd.

Earnhardt drove my car in the sportsman race and he was happy with the way it handled. I had run that car in a million short-track races and it was a good car. I run that car on short tracks when I won the Grand National East Championship in 1972. Afterwards he told Richard he liked that car better than anything he ever drove before. He felt like my superspeedway car would be a race winner and he'd like to have it. So it was already in our minds to put Dale Earnhardt in my Dodge next year for the 600.

The day after that sportsman race, on October 6, 1974, was the Winston Cup National 500. Neil was uncharacteristically at the back of field and had

After bouncing off Richard Childress' 96 on the left, Neil's 06 plows through the inside rail with Jim Vandiver's 31 as Joe Frasson in 18 and instigator Buddy Baker's 15 crash closest to the camera on October 6, 1974, in the National 400 in Charlotte (Neil Castles Family Collection).

some interesting company. Buddy Baker was forced to start at the rear because his car owner Bud Moore had knifed the tires they had qualified on in a dispute with Goodyear. Baker vowed he would be at the front in some impossibly few number of laps. Baker did not make it, and Neil was involved in one of the wildest crashes of his career. As Baker ripped through the field, he clobbered Dick Brooks in front of the main grandstand and started a frightening multicar pileup. Neil was in the middle of it.

Baker wrecked all of us on the second or third lap of the race. When I come sliding on that grass flying sideways, I run right dead into Richard Childress before I went through the inside guardrail with Jim Vandiver. I can remember seeing Childress' car and BOOM, there it went. Me and Childress always got along good.

The racing was still there, but getting smaller in Neil's rear view mirror. It was a beautiful life he had and Hollywood was footing most of the bill. Perhaps a factor in Neil's good fortune was his lack of vices that combined to ruin a lot of racing careers and lives in general.

When I was a youngster I smoked once in a while. I'd smoke a cigarette, but very seldom. I threw them down and never did smoke another one. Oh, you'll see me [with a cigarette] in an old photo, but I never considered myself a smoker. And I'd go out and drink a beer or two, but I wasn't no heavy drinker. Hell, if you dealt with Gene Granger, that reporter from Spartanburg, you had to drink beer.

Neil and Jean Castles were living well and building a nice country kingdom for themselves outside of Charlotte. But it was still a hectic existence, with Hollywood instead of NASCAR keeping him hopping.

I had a farm down there on Sullins Road and had two or three horses in a barn. I built a shop right behind the house and a three-car garage. I operated all my racecars out of that shop for a long time. Prior to that I had a service station rented and I used that shop. I built that barn 60 feet long and 36 feet wide. I put in 12 stables, 12 by 12, with a 12-foot drive through the middle. Had running water to every stall. The horse would stick his nose in the trough and it would fill up with water. I had automatic waterers for the horses.

You know and I know that if you've got a horse in a barn, he'll stand in

Seven. That Championship Feeling

one stall and go round and round and round and pee right in the middle of the floor til he makes a mud hole. So I dug out the middle of every stall before we built the barn to run outside piping to each stall and put a rock septic tank in the middle of every stall. When it got peed in, it would go through the piping out into the pasture. I didn't invent it, I just knew where the horses were going to pee.

I had three horses. Donna, my baby girl, had a horse, Jean had one, and I had a big red horse that was just like part of the family. I'd walk up to the fence anywhere I was at and holler at that horse and she'd just run up to the fence. I'd step up on the fence post and jump on the horse and I could ride that horse anywhere in the country and never put a saddle on it, never put a bridle on it, just ride it. I never held on to nothing. That horse was attached to me. Every which way I leaned, that's the way the horse went.

Incredible! Jean and Neil had built a horse palace and a showplace to raise their children.
But talking about the Sullins Road house brought back a bittersweet memory for Neil. In life you never know when to say goodbye to an old friend, and in auto racing it seems magnified.

Speedy Thompson was at my house on Sullins Road. You'd go in the back door and I had built a bar all the way across that kitchen with stools on both sides of it. If the guys in the shop wanted to come in the back door they could sit down there and have a drink or a bite to eat. Speedy Thompson come in there and I give him a right front shock, a left rear shock, and a right rear spring for his car to run at Charlotte the next day. Well, that was the kinds of friends we'd been for years. I had to go somewhere to a race myself. When the race was over they told me that Speedy was dead. He died of a heart attack in the racecar.

During a caution flag of a sportsman race at the old Charlotte Fairgrounds on April 2, 1972, Speedy Thompson pitted and told his crew chief he did not feel well, but would cool off under the caution and "get some fresh air." When the race restarted, Speedy's Camaro hit the fourth turn guardrail after he had a seizure, and the first person to win a stock car race at a 100 miles per hour average was gone on the day before his 46th birthday. Neil Castles and Speedy Thompson had been close friends since the midget and modified racing days of the early 1950s.

With his own racing career winding down by 1975, Neil had agreed the previous fall with Charlotte Motor Speedway owner Richard Howard to put Dale Earnhardt in one of his Dodges for the World 600, a southern Memorial Day tradition. But things were cooking under the surface and were not as they appeared.

Ed Negre come to me and said, "Neil, would you sell that other car you've got?" "Well, I hadn't thought about it or planned on it." He said, "I want to buy it." I said, "Well, Ed, I've always tried to help you out when I could. If you need it, I'll sell it to you." Ed said, "Then let's come to terms on it and I'll buy it." So I agreed to sell it to him for basically what it was worth. Ed's son Norman come and picked the car up and took it home with him. He had it painted blue with those yellow 8s on it overnight. He wanted my name off of it and made an Ed Negre car out of it right away.

I called Ed and said, "When are you going to pay me for that car?" "Why, I've got the money coming. I'll have it for you in a day or two." Come to find out that he knew I had a deal with Richard Howard to put Dale Earnhardt in a car for the 600. He went and told Richard that he had bought the car from me. Ed told Richard not to pay me any money. He needed for Richard to pay him so he could pay me for the car. So Richard called me and said that Ed was over there trying to get him [Richard] to pay him [Ed] for the car. I said, "Well, did you give him the money?" "Yes." Ed got the money, Ed got the car, and Ed got the whole ball of wax. He collected the money from Richard, never paid me a nickel, and kept the car. Never got paid a nickel! So I asked [his son] Norman for the car back. Norman said, "Well, that was between you and Daddy," and he went the hell back to where he come from. Ed had all kinds of problems.

His wife and Jean were good friends and sat in the scoring stand together and everything. She come to score the race and was all upset and tore up. Jean wanted to know what in the world had happened. She said, "A girl showed up at my house one morning at six o'clock with a baby and said it was Ed's. He ain't paid me nothing to take care of it and I want the money." Well, that threw a monkey wrench in a lot of friendships with that deal. He did a lot of things that he got away with because a lot of people like me liked him. He was from northern California where all them big redwood trees grow and they cut all that big timber. He had trucks that hauled that timber. That's what he was doing.

Seven. That Championship Feeling

Neil looks back on the whole Howard-Earnhardt-Negre episode nostalgically.

That's part of life. Dale Earnhardt was in a Dodge Charger that I was selling to Ed Negre. I never got paid for it and Dale Earnhardt drove it in his first Winston Cup race. So Dale Earnhardt drove my car in his first race.

For the World 600 on May 25, 1975, Dale Earnhardt qualified the car 33rd and completed 355 of the 400-lapper for 22nd place. Finishing right behind Earnhardt was his future boss and six-time championship car owner Richard Childress. But the Dodge was no longer Neil's familiar red and white number 06, but the blue and yellow number 8 of Ed Negre. History records—and race fans, especially those millions of Dale Earnhardt's, will always respond—that The Intimidator got his first Cup start in an Ed Negre Dodge. Let it be known that the car did and still does, wherever it is, belong to Neil Castles.

Neil did attempt to get Ed Negre to pay up, but it still never happened. Never will, either. Ed Negre passed away on June 4, 2014.

I jumped him four or five times about it, but he took off back to where he came from. I found out recently that Norman's dead. He never raced, he just worked on his daddy's racecar. He started building roll cages and doing fabrication. He did a lot of fabrication work, cutting down fenders where we were cheating.

A little-known fact is that Richard Howard and Neil Castles did get together to put another up-and-coming racer in the 600 field in 1975. Making his fifth career start in the Big Chance Special number 06 Chevrolet was 35-year-old Harry Gant out of Taylorsville, North Carolina, who qualified a splendid 11th, but dropped out with engine trouble for 31st.

Although Neil hardly ever went to Hollywood, California, for movie-related work, he did go there to race, and had a nostalgic encounter with an old movie acquaintance in Tinsel Town.

When I went out there I spent more time at Riverside because we went out there to race twice a year. Me, Jean, my mother, all the kids were staying in a big motel in downtown Riverside and there came the awfullest rainstorm you've ever seen. California's good for it. Well, it rained for four or five days straight. From the motel all the way to the racetrack right up the mountains it

Neil "Soapy" Castles

washed all these oranges down that road. It was solid full oranges and they were bouncing down through there as far as you could see. It put the race out of business for a week. So we took the kids and went to Universal Studios and watched them filming *Gilligan's Island*. And of course the Skipper was Alan Hale, Jr., my old friend from *Thunder in Carolina*. He remembered me and we got along real good as before. There were a lot of people that got used in one movie and we would bring them back for more. Actors and technical people.

The racing was about over for Neil, both as a driver and an owner. Neil Castles gave a real stock car legend his last two rides in 1976. In 2016, he became a member of the NASCAR Hall of Fame.

I never really decided to retire from racing. I just ran out of cars and money. The last races that I went to was at Rockingham and Charlotte. Richard Howard was determined to get Bobby Isaac in a car. Isaac had been sick for a while and he knew it. Cotton had my car in Rockingham because Richard wanted Isaac to drive the car there. I hired Cotton and his crew pitted the car and I think we finished sixth. He was sick at Charlotte for the 600. Richard said he was going to drive that car if it was the last thing he ever did. It almost was! We left the drivers' meeting walking back towards the car and Isaac said to me, "You go straight to that truck and put on your uniform because I ain't going to wait on the first caution flag. I'm coming down the pit road and you get in the car." He run three laps, hit the clutch, and blowed the engine. He blowed the engine to get out of feeling guilty to Richard. That damn engine was worth $75,000. It was a brand-new Junior Johnson engine and he did it on purpose because he knew he was going to die. He was at Hickory, got out of a racecar, went over and sat down by the fence and died.

The records reflect that in his penultimate start, Bobby Isaac drove what was listed as Richard Howard's number 6 Chevrolet on Leap Year Day, February 29, 1976, in the Carolina 500 at North Carolina Motor Speedway in Rockingham. Isaac started 13th, finishing sixth in what was actually Neil's car that Howard was sponsoring. It was the 1970 and inaugural Winston Cup Champion's final top ten. The finale was on Memorial Day, May 30, 1976, at the Charlotte Motor Speedway and the World 600 in the same car. His health failing, the old war horse started 34th and blew the engine on the 39th of 400 laps for 38th place. Neil was standing by in his uniform ready for the relief job that never came. Two and a half months later, on August 13, 1976, forty-three-year-

Seven. That Championship Feeling

old Bobby Isaac climbed out of a sportsman car running fourth at Hickory Speedway, collapsed, rallied a bit, and passed away just after midnight in the hospital with his family and new wife of three weeks. He was voted into the NASCAR Hall of Fame Class of 2016.

Neil Castles briefly sums up what happened to Neil Castles.

I got involved with the movies through the racing and one just over time replaced the other. I had a choice of keeping my job with the movie company or try to come up with a new racecar. I kept my job at the movie company and drove *different* cars.

From the early 1950s with Buddy Shuman, the Colvins, the trip to England, the midgets and sprint cars, the modifieds and sportsman cars, countless qualifying and consolation races, and in 582 Convertible Division, Grand National, Grand National East, and Winston Cup Series races from 1957 through 1976, Neil was all done behind the wheel as a competitive racer. He wound up finishing in the top

It appears Neil Castles is looking to the future with his auto racing days behind him. A new life of stunts, movie sets, and Hollywood stars lay ahead (Neil Castles Family Collection).

ten in those races 35 percent of the time with a career-high fourth in the 1969 Grand National Standings. He was the inaugural Grand National East Champion in 1972 with two wins and in the top ten all but once. He helped fellow racers race, not to mention aiding sick kids and nuns, without hesitation. He risked his life unnecessarily without a windshield when others would have quit immediately. He was witness to unthinkable horror many times, lost close friends, some crashing with him, and escaped from the hospital the only time he was injured badly enough to be in one. With his loving and supportive wife Jean by his side nearly every step of the way, Neil "Soapy" Castles hung up the helmet and goggles for good in 1976 and set out on another decades-long adventure where he continued to risk his life, this time among the stars.

Eight

Lights, Camera and Lots of Action

In 1976 the racing was over. For a decade already, Neil Castles had become increasingly in demand as a stunt man and consultant in the making of motion pictures and television productions. He had performed stunts for years and has no idea of how many, when, or where they all took place. During his racing career he had been credited and uncredited for his work in Thunder Road, Thunder In Carolina *(where he also had a speaking part),* Death at the Stock Car Races, *and* Speedway, *in which he was paid to be Elvis Presley's double. If all that was not enough, now it was time to get serious about working in the movies. No more dividing time with auto racing. Hollywood called and Neil Castles answered.*

In early 1977, Neil Castles was approached by a much-respected actor, writer, and director about his possible participation in a major Hollywood motion picture. Not just any Hollywood motion picture, but one about Neil's sport and a longtime friend and competitor.

Jean and I lived up at the lake. This guy came up there, a black guy, and rang the doorbell. He said, "Neil, my name is Melvin Van Peebles. I'm here to see you and talk to you about doing a movie." That's when we sat down in the living room and decided to do *Greased Lightning*. I agreed to furnish the cars, do as many stunts as I saw fit to do, and provide crash cars when we needed them. I had to have all flathead Fords, you see. I told him that I could put it together. He said, "What do you think it's going to cost?" "I have no idea. We'll take it a day at a time. I'll tell you how many cars I can get, what it's going to cost for them, and where we're going to get them from." He said, "Do you think you can find enough people to let you have the cars?" I said, "We're going to have to buy them. Most of them are outdated and we're going to have to work on them." Melvin said, "Well, we want to put Richard Pryor in a Ford flathead."

Eight. Lights, Camera and Lots of Action

Lobby card for *Greased Lightning*, in which Neil Castles wore numerous hats including car finder, stunt man, mediator, set decorator, and paymaster (Internet).

So Neil went to work on the Third World Cinema/Warner Brothers production of Greased Lightning. *The movie stars Richard Pryor as Wendell Scott, glamorous Pam Grier as Wendell's wife Mary, and others including two-time Golden Globe winner Beau Bridges,* Blazing Saddles *and* Vanishing Point *star Cleavon Little, Woodstock veteran Richie Havens, two-time Oscar nominee Vincent Gardenia, Georgia politicians Julian Bond and Maynard Jackson, and the movie's villain Earl Hindman. Hindman's best-known role was probably as the neighbor who never showed his whole face on the sitcom* Home Improvement. *Much had to be done, and first was the acquisition of a fleet of authentic flathead Fords and other racecars that were raced in the early 1950s. Neil knew exactly where to go.*

So Nicky Miller in Asheville had two '56 Ford flathead modifieds. I called Nicky and said, "I want them cars." He said, "Well, I don't want to sell them."

Neil "Soapy" Castles

"Yeah you do. Just tell me what you want." He said, "I know you want them for that movie you're working on." I said, "I do. I'll tell you what I'll do. I'll pay you so much a week rent on them and I'll pay you this for them when it's over with and you can have the two cars junked back." I rented them, then I bought them.

We painted those two '56 Fords of Nicky Miller and matched them. We put them side by side and I had Nicky match the paint on them and make identical cars, then we took them to Athens, Georgia. I had to have flathead cars and Melvin Van Peebles was the producer and the director. When he wanted something he came to me and told me what he wanted. He said, "We have to have this may cars all different numbers and colors just like they'd been at that time."

Neil had the two lead cars for Richard Pryor as Wendell Scott to drive, but still needed a dozen or so more. No problem.

The only person I knew that dealt that close with that many cars was Mel Joseph in Dover, Delaware, that built the Dover Speedway. Mel and I had been friends for years. He had a landing strip in his backyard that you could land a jet on. He kept a twin engine plane in his carport. I called Mel and I said, "How many of these flathead cars can you come up with?" "How many do you want?" I told him. He said, "I'll get back to you." He called me back and said, "I've got these cars lined up and they'll be parked up the street from my business on a vacant lot where we can load them on tractor trailers." I said, "You put a price on them and I'll bring a suitcase full of $100 bills." I went to the office and I told Melvin, "I don't know how much I'm going to spend, but I want a suitcase full of $100 bills." And that's what I got.

I had a charter plane waiting on me all the time. Me, Jean, and Little Neil went and got on the plane and landed in Mel's backyard. We got off the plane and got in a car with Mel and went down there to a whole field lined up full of damn cars. So we started figuring what it would cost to buy each one of these and this, that, and the other.

The wrecker driver that was bringing them in and loading them said, "I got to get another one over here," and I said, "I'm going over here to see another one." I followed him over there and he hooked it up to the wrecker and we came across a little old narrow road and he lost it off the back of the wrecker. It went down through the woods and down through a cornfield, a big cornfield with stalks as tall as I was. I pulled over and got out of the car

Eight. Lights, Camera and Lots of Action

and went down there. I came back and got in the car and Jean said, "How bad is it torn up?" I said, "Honey, it ain't hurt at all, but it must have 20 bushels of corn in it." So that boy pulled it out of the bushes and carried it over there and dumped the corn out of it. We took it to Georgia and put a new grille in it where the corn eat it up.

Neil acquired the necessary racecars and got them transported to Athens, Georgia, where the racing scenes from early in Wendell's career were to be shot. It remained to be seen if the star, Richard Pryor, could hold up his end of the project as a racecar driver.

The two cars I got from Nicky Miller and painted up were the two key cars, a backup car and a principle car. Melvin came down there and said, "Now, he's going to be here this evening and he wants to see that car. Richard Pryor wants to see what it looks like." So they went to the airport and picked him up and brought him out there to the racetrack in Athens.

Pryor came down there and looked at it and I showed him how you cranked it and he said, "Well, these are just little toy cars." I said, "No they ain't! They're more than you think they are." He said, "Well, I can drive a straight drive car. I've been driving a straight drive car all my life." He got in it and sat down. I said, "If you're going to try to crank it up and drive it, you're going to have to fasten your seat belt." So I put the seat belt on him. He made two laps and went down in one and two and end over end he went. Tore that car all to hell. All it did was get a little red mud on him and change his color.

The star of the show wrecked one of the racecars he had called a "toy car." It was obviously a very dangerous toy. No problem for Neil. He needed that car and handled it in stride.

Now I don't have a backup car and I can't trust him in the other one. But I don't think he wanted to get back in the car right then anyway. Later on, I had a car, an old blue Ford, that I drove the whole movie. I bought it in Delaware and it was a good running car. I got the chassis where I could go down and pitch it in the corner like a midget and pick that left front wheel up, get in the gas, and go on. Well, I run side by side with Pryor to keep him straight to do the movie.

On both sides of the camera, Neil was hard at work. This time, IMDb lists

Neil "Soapy" Castles

him Stunt Driver *along with Ted Duncan as Stunt Coordinator and Ernest Robinson as Stunt Coordinator/Stunt Double: Richard Pryor. And there is also Greased Lightning's villain named Beau Welles.*

The bad guy that was in the movie was a New York actor named Earl Hindman. He had never driven in a car in his life and didn't know nothing. All he told me was, "Everywhere I go I ride in the back of a taxi." He couldn't drive nothing. I've got pictures of them putting a mustache on me to double for him. I had to double for the white guy from New York. There's a picture of them putting makeup on me, whiskers and beard, and G.C. Spencer is standing behind me laughing like hell.

After being told that Athens Speedway would not pass the production people's vision of a racetrack in the 1950s in the condition it was in, Neil again sprang into action. As usual, he knew exactly who to call.

Now were getting down to filming this movie and we've got to have plenty of decorations. So I called T. Wayne Robertson, the Winston guy, and told him what I needed, how I needed it, and what I wanted. T. Wayne said, "Don't worry. I'll have a crew there to decorate the racetrack." He sent a crew down there and decorated that thing for Winston. That's the only thing you could see in there was Firestone and Winston. We decorated that thing on Saturday. Everybody was happy, but a few people.

Of all the hats and helmets Neil Castles had to wear, the trickiest was that of handling the needs of the subject of Greased Lightning, *Wendell Scott. Wendell enlisted the assistance of an unwanted outsider and the fun began.*

Neil made up to double for actor Earl Hindman, the bad guy in *Greased Lightning* in 1977 at Middle Georgia Raceway in Byron. Amused racer G.C. Spencer is at the right (Neil Castles Family Collection).

140

Eight. Lights, Camera and Lots of Action

Down there on that movie, they wanted to know if I got along with Wendell. I said, "Yeah." The production people said, "We'll take care of Wendell, whatever he needs. You just provide the cars, do the driving, crash whatever needs to be crashed, just keep us updated on what we've got to do." So we got down to where I had to make a deal with Wendell, but Wendell and Melvin Van Peebles fell out. Wendell came up with a black New York lawyer that weighed about 400 pounds and Wendell started demanding two or three million dollars. I told Wendell, "You can forget it, Wendell. You ain't getting that kind of money." Wendell's son was in the penitentiary in Atlanta for dope at that time. He said, "I want that boy out of jail. It's going to cost a lot of money and I need the money." I said, "I don't know whether I can get him out of jail or not, but I will make you some money. How about I hire you to drive for me and double for Pryor until I decide what I want to do?" So I started paying him a weekly salary just to drive a lap or two here and a lap or two there. I finally told Wendell, "I'll just buy that old car that you've got that I need to finish the movie down there in Byron, Georgia, at that half-mile asphalt." They once found a liquor still underneath it and that's where we were going to finish the movie.

Neil got Wendell some money. Lots of money. But for Wendell's New York mouthpiece, there was a problem.

Wendell was wanting money. Production gave me a check made out to Wendell for a large sum of money. They said, "Go give that check to him, get him to sign these releases, and get rid of that lawyer." So I went down there and met with Wendell and the lawyer in the motel room. I gave Wendell the check and he handed it to that lawyer. The lawyer said, "Now that ain't nothing. You ain't signing nothing for that." I said, "Give me the check." Wendell said, "Let's think on this." I said, "I'll keep the check until morning and if you want the check let me know. That's a lot of money, Wendell. You've never seen that much money and you ain't going to see it again." That lawyer said, "That won't even pay my motel expenses." I told that New York lawyer, "The best thing you can do is go back where you come from."

And he did. With that unexpected problem on a plane back to the Big Apple, negotiations with Wendell were resumed.

So Wendell agreed that he'd probably be better off taking that check. I said, "No, Wendell, I've done tore that check up. You can forget that." He said,

Neil "Soapy" Castles

"You mean I ain't getting nothing?" I said, "I'm going to pay you a day's pay for driving that car." "What about the money?" I told him, "You had it in your hand and you threw it away. Now I've done tore the check up." He said, "What are you going to do about it? You can't get it back?" "Hell no! You've done screwed that up. I'll have to go back to production and have them write you a new check." Wendell said, "I'll be glad to take that check and sign anything you want." I said, "I'll bring you a check in the morning and have the production office fill out the papers." So I went down there in the morning and they burned him a check and he signed the papers and agreed to drive the car. The check was for $100,000. Production wrote the check, I didn't. He got his kid out of jail with it.

Another racing movie expense one might not realize was essential for auto racing itself. Tires.

I had to have a tire service. Well, Goodyear would not talk to me at all about tires. They didn't have any use for me. So Gene White had the Firestone distributorship in Atlanta. I had Gene bring me two Firestone trucks, two stacks of tires, and four guys mounting tires. He came down and set up in the pits and I had a complete tire service just like at any other Grand National race.

Neil flashes back to the reason he had a falling out with the Goodyear Tire and Rubber Company many years earlier.

What happened to me and Goodyear was when I went to Darlington with my '56 Ford to qualify. We had to buy recapped tires from Ross Huggins up there in Greensboro, North Carolina. Recapped tires were the only tires we could buy at Darlington to qualify on. I didn't like the idea of running that convertible at Darlington on recapped tires qualifying at a hundred and something miles an hour. So I put me on four damn recaps and qualified for the race. It was all well and good. After it come to play in 1959 that I was going to make *Thunder in Carolina*, Goodyear started getting very friendly. They see that Crash Grant took over Goodyear from Ross Huggins. We had '57 Chevrolets that we were going to use and we had to buy tires from Huggins to put on them. All at once Goodyear jumped up and said, "We're going to donate you all the tires." I was pissed at them to start with. Me and Crash Grant took two sets of tires to the Darlington Motel and rolled them in our room we stayed in. We stayed up all night and we painted them Goodyear tires white letter. Nobody had ever seen a white letter tire. Me and Crash painted all them tires. When I rolled them out on those movie cars and they saw those white letters, they liked to went through the damn ceiling. What they didn't like was that they didn't get any credit for it whatsoever. Me and Crash did it and they wanted big credit for painting those tires white letter. I shot them in the ass when I did it. From then on, Goodyear wouldn't even talk to me. So that's when I started painting tires to get even with them.

Neil Castles startled the tire people with his handmade white letter tires. It was also a surprise to find out that a director change had taken place. His opening demands were off-the-charts unreasonable, but Neil very diplomatically handled it.

They decided that they didn't like Melvin Van Peebles' dealings and they fired him and brought in Michael Schultz. He didn't know the front bumper of a racecar from the back. Michael came down to the shop and said, "Those cars aren't running fast enough. I don't want them. I want you to go to Chevrolet and get Chevrolet engines and take the Ford motors out." I said "OK, in the morning we'll do that. I'll go to Atlanta General Motors." I went to Atlanta General Motors and talked to them in the morning and said that I needed this many engines for this many cars. "I'm going to need bell housing adapters, this, that, and the other, and put a price on it. I'll call you in the morning. I'll have a truck there to load the stuff." I went in there and told Michael what it was going to cost him. "Oh, we can't do that." I said, "No we can't. *You're* going to do it because *you're* the one that made this deal." I said, "Do you want to pay General Motors this price for them engines? Do you want me to send a truck down there to get them?" He said, "Well, maybe you can tune the cars up so they'll look like they're running a little better." So I put Nicky Miller and his crew working on them and we had our lead cars where they worked fine. I had sent that Nicky Miller car that Richard Pryor flipped to a body shop in Asheville and had them redo it and put it on the frame machine. When the thing was over I told Nicky, "Load them cars up and take them home."

Michael Schultz was a veteran African American director already with well-known television and silver screen credits such as The Rockford Files, Cooley High, Starsky and Hutch, Baretta, Movin' On, *and* Car Wash, *then*

Neil "Soapy" Castles

later Which Way Is Up?, Sgt. Pepper's Lonely Hearts Club Band, L.A. Law, Picket Fences, Chicago Hope, Ally McBeal, Touched by an Angel, *and as of this writing* Black-ish. *Needless to say, the man can direct.*

So we got down to the nitty-gritty and I told Wendell, "Don't bring your old racecar down here because I can't use it now." He was going to be driving the Grand National car. Well, I had to drive the other car, and that just so happened to be one of the cars that belonged to Jim Vandiver. I had called Vandiver and everybody I knew that had Grand National cars. Well, I jumped in his Dodge and I was at home in there. And I had to put Wendell in his Chevrolet to do it.

In July of 1977, the movie Greased Lightning *premiered across the country. According to IMDb, it ranks 116th of 2,905 titles produced that year. Whether it was a financial success depends on whose bookkeeping you want to believe. According to author Brian Donovan in his Wendell Scott biography* Hard Driving, *Scott received a down payment of $25,000 and percentage of the profits. As was later explained to him, Wendell should have agreed to a percentage of the gross, not the profits. Movies often do not show profits as a way for studios to not have to pay "outsiders." Wendell Scott was disappointed with the financial windfall not being as large he had expected it to be. However, it appears Neil did everything he could for Wendell and successfully fulfilled all the various aspects of the production thrown his way by Hollywood.*

One veteran stunt man who stands out to Neil during his career was Everett Creach. Creach, as Neil calls him, was about Neil's same age. He is listed with 90 movies going back to My Friend Flicka *in 1943 when he was ten years old. Some of his other credits and uncredits are* She Wore a Yellow Ribbon, How the West Was Won, The Green Berets, Tora! Tora! Tora!, Dirty Harry, Diamonds Are Forever, The Towering Inferno, Young Guns, *and dozens of others until the year of his death in 1994.*

Neil explains about the integral parts of movie making: stunt coordinator, picture cars, and transportation coordinator. Neil explains what they are.

Everett Creach was one of the most recognized stunt coordinators in Hollywood. I worked with Creach more than anybody. Anytime they had something going on, some kind of driving stunt that needed doing, he'd just call me and I'd go do it. I worked with Creach for years. I got pictures of us working together when we did that thing in Tennessee, *What Comes Around,*

Eight. Lights, Camera and Lots of Action

with Jerry Reed in 1985. Hell, Jerry Reed and Neil, Jr., wore out a set of tires out on a Blazer going around a racetrack. Creach would also call and ask where they could find such and such a car and what will it take to get it. I'd go out and find the cars and get them.

When you turn on the TV or see a movie and you see cars, all of those cars have to be provided by somebody. Those are called picture cars. Like in the movie *Leatherheads* with [George] Clooney. That was a football movie about 1920s football. We had a hundred and something T-Models on that show. I got all of Alex Beam's and all I could gather up. I got all the T-Models that you could think of to do that thing *Leatherheads* that they filmed in Spartanburg. All of those T-Models I furnished. Part of them were Alex's and part of them I drove in from everywhere. You couldn't find a hundred people to drive the damn things. I had to get enough people and teach them to drive them to do the chase scenes with them T-Models. I was there every day. All those old cars I was responsible for getting them down there and getting them took care of. When you see chase scenes, wrecks, cars demolished, all of them are picture cars. I had a fleet of police cars, a fleet of taxicabs, all those old New York Yellow Cabs were actually old model Ford chassis. We had to dig up some of that stuff. One of the buses on there was one of the buses they used on *The Waltons*. We shipped it in, used it, and sent it back. This is all the job of the transportation coordinator.

The transportation coordinator is in charge of anything that rolls a wheel. That's what my son Neil, Jr., does. He's the transportation coordinator on a movie in Atlanta right now. He hires people like me to get the cars and get the stuff done. That includes air transportation and production approves it. It's a big operation. Every movie has ten or 15 vans. You got hair, makeup, wardrobe, all of these people that are staying in a motel or a hotel, or wherever they put you. In the mornings, somebody has to pick them up and take them straight to the set. We have caterers set up with huge tents or buildings that feed everybody at a certain time every morning. So you got 15 van drivers doing nothing but hauling people and actors. We got wardrobe people that bring in a tractor and trailer full of wardrobes like we did in that war picture we made in South Carolina, *The Patriot*. All of them people running up and down that hill getting shot, all them uniforms had to be sent to the cleaners and cleaned overnight and back at the set to go on actors in the morning. Like everything that construction had, we had to use to build that town, build that church, and all that stuff. We had ten stake-bed truck drivers that don't do nothing but haul lumber, material, and whatever you need. And if you got a lot of different locations, you got people driving stake-beds running between locations hauling stuff they've got to have. They say, "Call transportation and get such and such and put it on a stake-bed and send it to me." We were in Asheville on top of that mountain and I took a job driving a van. It paid union scale, Teamster, everything, and there was no stunt work in it.

I still deal with all kinds of cars. People needing cars are calling me all the time. I'm still dealing with picture cars. I just went to Mooresville the other day and took a T-Model from down there at Alex Beam's. We got it out and got it running. You've got to be a mechanic if you're going to run a T-Model. I still fool with T-Models and some flat-head Ford stuff.

I was working on *Six Pack* and Creach was the stunt coordinator. I could not do the stunt work on that show unless I got a SAG card for that particular job. I'd had one previously for some TV stuff, but I don't even know what happened to it. It was here and gone. Anyway, I went and got a SAG card to do the driving on that thing with Kenny Rogers. Kenny was in that old model car and I had two modified dirt cars. I rigged the chassis on my car where I could go down underneath Kenny, lay the right front wheel up on the running board, go down into the corner and slide it off and never touch him. You do two or three of those and they don't have to ask where you come from, just when can you do it. But you get a SAG card based on your reputation, the director you're dealing with. There was a lot of pressure on me on *Greased Lightning* because it was SAG, but it wasn't SAG, but it was, but it wasn't. I had a temporary one. Hell, we just did what we needed to do to do the movie and went on.

The difficult-to-obtain and oh-so-necessary SAG card needed to ensure proper credit and residual pay for work in film, television, and radio (Neil Castles Family Collection).

The Academy Awards are voted on by the members of the Academy of Motion Picture Arts and Sciences, and they first awarded the Oscars in 1929. The Hollywood Foreign Press Association votes on the best in motion pictures and later television and have awarded the Golden Globes since 1943. The Screen Actors Guild–American Federation of Television and Radio Artists

Eight. Lights, Camera and Lots of Action

vote on the outstanding performances in movies and prime time television and have awarded a statuette called the Actor since 1995. Naturally, one of the duties of being a SAG member is voting for the SAG Awards. Neil is inundated with DVDs each year for his consideration. It used to be VHS tapes, which take up enormously more space.

I've got tons of DVDs down in the basement. I'll be glad to donate you a few hundred if you want them. I'm on the nominating committee for the Screen Actors Guild still after all these years. If you make a movie and you want somebody as dumb as I am to nominate it, send me a copy of it. If I like it, I'll nominate it. We've got boxes of them from this year and years past. I just hate to throw them away. Some of them anyway.

One of the more notable and beloved celebrities Neil ever worked with was a fellow North Carolinian who became a very close friend in 1986 until his death. Originally from Mount Airy, North Carolina, by way of Mayberry, Andy Samuel Griffith.

I worked five years on *Matlock*. Andy Griffith loved antique cars. I was in Wilmington working on a movie. I don't even know what it was. Neil Hyman was the transportation coordinator of a movie that I'd worked on down there. He caught me by the shirt and said, "I got Andy Griffith coming in here from California. They just sent his motorhome in here. He's bad to deal with. He's fired the last ten or 12 drivers he's had. I need somebody that can drive that motorhome in a hurry. I know you've run a motorhome all over this country. Would you drive a motorhome for me for a little bit to get it started?" I said, "I'll try it for a couple of days and if it works out, good. If it don't, he can go on up the road and I will, too. When do we leave, next 30 minutes?" He said, "Probably eight o'clock tonight."

He handed me the keys to a new Lincoln and I went to the airport and picked Andy up and took him to the residence that they'd rented for him. After I dropped him off, I went back and picked him up and took him to the studio to introduce him. They made a little production out of it and I took him back home. Came back and they were setting up the first day of filming.

I went back there and looked at that old motorhome and it was a dog if I'd ever seen one. I told Neil Hyman, "This thing was worn out before it ever left California. It ain't going to be nothing but trouble." We got the generator and the air running, fixed everything on it.

Two days later, we came to the studio, got in the motorhome, and we went down to Southport, North Carolina, and filmed the whole day there. We come back to the studio, got out, and they sent me over to the Ford place and I picked up a new Ford Explorer and gave it to Andy to drive from the studio home and back every day. You couldn't take that motorhome back to where he was living.

Finally he moved up to Figure Eight Island, right above Wilmington. If you go to the end of Wrightsville Beach and look right straight across, that's Figure Eight Island. He had two Model As, a T-Model, a '46 Ford convertible, his wife had a '57 Thunderbird convertible, and he had a '32 Ford truck he drove to the grocery store and back every day. This is when he lived at the beach.

Andy Griffith had a passion for antique cars and there was one in particular that he wanted to find. As luck would have it, he was hanging out with the best car finder in the land.

He got to talking to me about old cars and he wanted him an old Packard. Nothing else would do. He had to have an old Packard. He dealt with that

The 1937 Packard sought after by Andy Griffith that Neil located, seen here on a movie lot in Wilmington, North Carolina, circa 1990 (Neil Castles Family Collection).

Eight. Lights, Camera and Lots of Action

dude in Reno that had all the antique cars. He had about 20 antique Packards. He was a collector. So Andy wanted a Packard. In the meantime, he had a Model A four-door Phaeton and wanted the engine changed to a Model B engine so that it would run faster up the only hill on Manteo Island. So I went down to his house and brought one of them back to the shop. I had the machine shop that built things for me machine the block. We built a new engine for that Model A, stuck it in it, and took it to the studio. Oh, that was wonderful. So I sent it to an upholstery shop in Greenville, South Carolina, and had them redo the upholstery in it. That was his ride right there. He didn't want anything to happen to that. I wrapped the original engine in plastic and took it to his house and left it in the garage so he would have the original engine if he ever decided to sell the car. But Andy had to have a Packard.

As always, Neil's decades of experience and friendships took him down the road to exactly what Andy wanted.

Miller Beer Company had a Packard that was once owned by the Mafia that they used in parades to promote Miller Beer. Don Miller owns the Miller Racing Team in Mooresville. I sat down and talked to him and asked him where that Packard was. He said, "Back there in the back of the building." We went back there and looked at it. I called Andy and told him. Andy kept a plane waiting on him any time he wanted it. I picked him up at the airport and we went back there and looked at that Packard. He looked at it and said, "Let's go get me back to the airplane." We started out the door and Don said, "Andy, do you think you'd like to have that car?" He said, "I'd like to have it. Put a price on it." He did and Andy said, "Well, I'll just write you a check," and handed it to him.

So I went up there and picked the car up three days later, took it to the Wilmington studio, and me and Neil, Jr., cranked it up and drove it all over the studio. Andy rode all over the studio and Wilmington with it. It was a four-door convertible. It was a '37 or '38. He wanted it redone. I took it to New York and had it restored, but when I got it back from New York, Andy was not happy with the job they had done on the Packard. So Andy had Neil Jr., and I take it to Reno and have a shop that Andy's longtime friend Bill Harrah used to restore the car. But Andy was a great guy and one day all these Hooters girls came down there and we all had dinner on the set.

Neil "Soapy" Castles

Andy Griffith might have been hard to handle to some people, but Neil Castles was, and still is for that matter, as easygoing as they come. The other drivers Andy had to deal with probably felt intimidated and pressured by the mega-star, but Neil was immune to pressure of any kind. Whether performing death-defying stunts or hobnobbing with celebrities, Neil was at ease at all times and Andy Griffith was just another co-worker with whom he was making movies. He was also a good friend.

Not too far down the road from Neil and Jean lived a gentleman with some very high aspirations, and truth be told, he did very well for himself. According to IMDb he is known as the "Dixie DeMille" and got started in 1973 with a movie named Challenge. *Neil Castles was right there with him.*

I was doing movie and picture car work. I owned a marina and was doing just small independent movie stuff because I could provide the cars that they couldn't find. There was a guy in Shelby, North Carolina, that owned a tool and die company, Earl Owensby. He opened a studio up there somewhere around Boiling Springs, North Carolina, and was going into the movie business. Well, he wanted to make a movie and I made the first one for him. I furnished the cars, done the driving, and most of all the stunt work there was to be done. He wrote the script. It was called *Challenge*. I acted in it, too. I've got pictures of me beating the hell out of him at the Holiday Inn. There was so much blood they couldn't show it. There was a Pantera that I had in that movie and we had an airplane that we crashed at the end of the runway and burned it. I also burned a house down.

One of Neil's closest calls came during the filming of Challenge *in a brand-new car.*

I had a yellow $15,000 Pantera on Interstate 40 coming to the 221 exit and there was a pond of water in the fork there and it was very deep. The director said he'd love to see that car hit that pond of water. He told me to go down the Interstate, get off on the ramp, and hit that pond of water, and slide up the exit ramp. I said, "Well, let's make sure there ain't nothing in the water, no tree stumps, so I don't get hurt and tear up something 'cause I'm dealing with a very high-priced rear-engine car." So they got all the crew members down there to check out that water and make sure there was nothing in it that I was going to hit.

I had a Styrofoam pole where I came off Interstate 40, a road sign, right where I go up the ramp and that was to dead-center me over the water. I was

Eight. Lights, Camera and Lots of Action

Andy Griffith takes time out from filming *Matlock* to have lunch and pose with the local Hooters girls from Wilmington, North Carolina, circa 1990 (Neil Castles Family Collection).

running about 130 miles an hour when I hit that sign. We had Owensby's airplane in the air filming everything over it. Then I hit that water and it just exploded. The bottom of the seat I was sitting on threw me right up to the roof. And there was a concrete abutment in there and when I hit it, it went through the floor of the car and cut my billfold in two in my pocket. Now I'm sliding sideways up the exit ramp probably at still over 100 miles an hour. I ended

Fast friends during the shooting of *Matlock* and for years afterwards are a couple of North Carolina boys named Neil Castles and Andy Griffith (Neil Castles Family Collection).

up on Highway 221 going to Marion, North Carolina. I slid out in the road sideways and stopped on the other side of the road before it went in a ditch. The front end was gone, no suspension, and no steering to amount to anything.

When it landed on the other side, there was a motel on the right and Jean was to meet me there. Well, she had come a little early and didn't know I was going to wreck that damn car. I didn't intend to wreck it. I intended to split that water like an outboard motorboat. Jean was standing in the phone booth when I slid by her right out in the middle of 221.

But wait. There's more.

I got out of the car and Owensby said, "Well, you going to have to call John." I called John Holman that worked for me, no kin to the John Holman of Holman and Moody. He was a new car salesman at Burrs Lincoln Mercury in Charlotte. I had bought that car from him brand-new. I called him and said, "John, you got another one of them yellow Panteras?" He said. "Yeah." I said, "Where's it at? I just lost that first one." John said, "It came in on the convoy yesterday and I serviced it last night." I said, "Stick it on a truck and send it to me on 221." I told him where I was at and said, "Send that roll back so he take this other one 'cause it's torn all to hell." So he delivered the new one to me up on 221 and took the wrecked one back to my shop next to the house on Sullins Road. I told him to drop it at the end door next to the swimming pool. I had the body man at Burrs go out there and look at it and see if we were going to salvage it, fix it, or whatever. Within two hours of the time I tore that first car up, I had another new one. Those Pantera ran right at $15,000 apiece.

Another wild chase scene from Challenge *put Neil perilously close to serious injury or worse behind the wheel.*

We were on Interstate 70 coming down the mountain in the fall of the year and the tree leaves were on the ground a couple of inches deep. I was running through them in a Corvette sliding around those curves on Interstate 70 and we were doing it at a pretty good speed. So I hit them leaves and they were slick. I slid off the shoulder of the road and I hit a road sign first and it was to tell you that there was a 200-foot drop-off. When I got sideways it looked like I might go over the mountain. Right in the middle of the sound-

Eight. Lights, Camera and Lots of Action

man's tape this guy that worked for me, Kyle Lockhart, jumped up and yelled, "Oh, shit!" I was doing it on purpose, but I had got too far off the shoulder of the road and thought I was going to go 200 feet down the mountain. I missed it.

Challenge *was directed by Martin Beck and produced by Earl Owensby's E.O. Corporation and was released in October of 1974.*

Actually, 30 years or so after the fact, what we would find an extraordinary lifetime of memories all run together for Neil. Remembering specific incidents becomes very difficult and many of the movies seem to run together with flashes here and glimpses there of incidents from his past.

In *The Last American Hero*, I furnished most of the cars and about a quarter of the driving. I worked with Beau Bridges, who was also in *Greased

With others looking on, Neil Castles blasts a Corvette through a roadblock during the filming of *Challenge* near Shelby, North Carolina, in 1974 (Neil Castles Family Collection).

Lightning. What Comes Around I made in Nashville with Jerry Reed and was a short movie. I was a police [officer] in that movie and it was typical Jerry Reed. They bought a strip mall on the highway going into Nashville right behind a Union 76 station that had the first Cracker Barrel in the middle of it. It had a western store and all kinds of stores and we run a tractor trailer through it and burned the whole damn thing down. On *The Patriot* we had to have a bunch of van drivers to get all the people back and forth to the motel. I met Mel Gibson every day. We wrecked 20 cars down there in Wilmington on *Amos & Andrew* and nobody ever knew who wrecked them. Kenny Rogers was just a good guy. We got along well. We worked together the whole movie *Six Pack*. Never had no problems. All the people I've worked with all along I've never had any trouble with. And I never got more than a few bumps and bruises, but you had to prepare for that.

Speaking of Kenny Rogers, a big party was scheduled after shooting had wrapped for the day during Six Pack, *and of course Neil was invited.*

The Andy Griffith Show Reunion: Back to Mayberry, a 2003 television special, was shot in Wilmington, North Carolina. Neil Castles chatted with Opie Taylor, aka Ron Howard, during filming (Neil Castles Family Collection).

Eight. Lights, Camera and Lots of Action

We were in Atlanta making *Six Pack*. Prior to that, a couple of years earlier I had an ulcer in my stomach. I was losing a lot of blood internally and I was weak. So Jean, Susan, and Neil grabbed me up and took me to the hospital and they operated on me. Dr. Jett operated on it and went in there and think he left part of his tools in me. I never had any trouble with it for years. So we're in Georgia for *Six Pack* and I had been burning the candle at both ends. I got run down and started losing blood like before. I was weak and I was supposed to go to this big dinner at Kenny Rogers' house. We had just finished work and we were going from work to that party. I just walked in the office and told that girl, "Look, I don't feel good. Grab me a van. I need to go to the hospital." I seen I couldn't make it. I went to the hospital and they threw me on a table and I didn't know nothing for two days.

Neil missed the big party, but it probably saved his life.
Neil mentions briefly the digital effects of today and what is happening to the traditional stunt man.

Most of the stuff I did was with cars out on the highway. The only ones still making them good are some special effects people. The green screen fired a lot of people. There's not that much left for the stuntmen to do because of that green screen and all the phony-looking special effects.

Huge fiery explosions and cars careening crazily over the streets are more likely the handiwork of somebody toiling over a computer in Hollywood than a brave daredevil risking his own neck for the sake of realism.
Neil had one particular job that nearly turned out to be a movie reunion.

I worked with Claude Akins in *Movin' On*, a TV show where he was a truck driver and we filmed at the Charlotte Motor Speedway. All them championship trophies down there in my basement we used in that movie. When they were filming it some thieves stripped the mirrors off of the truck in the movie and tore it up. Well, they got up with me and got the truck put back together. There was a whole bunch of stuff between me and Claude. Rory Calhoun and Carey Loftin were in it too, and we used to go out to eat at the fish camp or steakhouse every night. It was great to see them again after we had worked together on *Thunder in Carolina* many years earlier.

Neil "Soapy" Castles

A couple of movie cops on the set of *The Summer of Ben Tyler*. **Neil Castles, Jr., left, with Neil Castles, Sr., right, posing in Burgaw, North Carolina, in 1996 (Neil Castles Family Collection).**

According to IMDb, a Movin' On *episode in 1975 called* The Big Wheel *aired on November 11, 1975, and along with Claude Akins starred Frank Converse, the other show regular, Rory Calhoun, Jo Ann Harris, Scott Brady, and Neil. Sixth billing is pretty good. Neil had a speaking role and played a character named Red Banning. Carey Loftin is listed under Stunts.*

Neil was always teaching actors how to drive a racecar to get them through a scene.

When we used them in a movie, I put them in a car and showed them what to do with it. I've done a lot of laps on the racetrack showing them what to do. I had Vandiver drive a dirt track for me. I had an extra car I had to do something with. Jim's always standing around saying, "What ya got going on?" So I'd put him in a car when I could.

In the late summer of 2001 Neil was working on a movie originally storyboarded as The Heist *directed by Gerard Pires, a Parisian making his only American movie. The movie climaxed on the New River Gorge Bridge near Fayetteville, West Virginia, which soars majestically 876 feet above the rocky*

Eight. Lights, Camera and Lots of Action

waters below. With a day to spare, everything was perfect to wrap up the shooting and get Neil back to Jean and their home in Charlotte. Everything was perfect except the timing.

The state police had the roads leading up that bridge blocked off. They hired me to do the cars and I had two police cars, a helicopter, and a tanker truck with fuel for the helicopter. I was a police [officer] and I brought my buddy up there from Wilmington to be the other police [officer] and bring a second police car. What was supposed to happen was these guys robbed the bank and the police was chasing them and I'm in the lead police car. Well, we crashed our cars on the bridge and they jumped out and as I drove towards them, they're standing out in the road shooting at me through my windshield. I run right at them and they seen I was going to run over them. Well, they were prepared for this anyway. They were all going to jump off the bridge. They had parachutes on. And about halfway down they were to open the parachutes and land in the river.

This was all happening on 9/11 and that hijacked plane crashed right there above us in Pennsylvania. I don't know what they were thinking, but the sheriff's department was handling everything. They grounded our helicopter that was going to shoot the scene from the air. Everything was on the ground. As soon as that plane crashed, they shut down everything on the bridge. The sheriff's department sent people under the bridge to make sure there hadn't been any dynamite placed there.

So much for being ahead of schedule. Needless to say, the United States did not know if it was under attack or not. In the grand scope of things, the movie shoot was vastly secondary in importance to national security. The movie crew had to regroup.

The sheriff's department carried us to the Holiday Inn to a meeting room to discuss the situation. Production said that due to you don't know what's going to happen to your family or nothing else, we're not going to demand that y'all stay here. "We'd like for you to stay here one more day. If you stay here one more day, we'll have enough in the can to call it a movie." They said to me, "Without you and your police cars to finish this thing up, we're out of business."

So I called Jean and talked to her on the phone. I told her I was in Charleston, West Virginia, at the Holiday Inn and I had agreed with these people to stay one more day. I said, "If you're afraid let me know and I'll have one of the kids to come stay with you." We didn't know that they were going to blow up the whole damn country or what. They had put that helicopter in the parking lot at the Holiday Inn.

Well, the next day we got a release from the sheriff's department that they could use the helicopter at the bridge only, 'cause they were scared of anything flying. So I stayed and finished the chase scenes with my police cars. My big part was I was as a police [officer] and I got paid as an actor every day.

Incredible! Filming on September 11, 2001, of all days. Although IMDb lists dozens of production companies for this movie and no domestic theatrical release, it premiered in France on May 8, 2002. The Heist morphed through several titles including Riders, Team Riders, High Risk, $teal, *and finally* Steal. *Whatever the name, it sounds like the stunts during that climax on the bridge would be worth the price of admission alone, especially now that the backstory is known.*

The film industry has largely gone away from North Carolina as the state legislature put an end to the incentives Hollywood had been offered to come

As a policeman, a popular role for Neil, he stands on the New River Gorge Bridge near Fayetteville, West Virginia, on that fateful day, September 11, 2001, during filming of *The Heist* (Neil Castles Family Collection).

Eight. Lights, Camera and Lots of Action

there and make movies in the first place. Here is Neil's version of what happened.

It was called the Incentive Plan. The Incentive Plan is where everything bought to make a movie in North Carolina you pay taxes on. Every nickel you spend, you pay taxes on it. At the end of the movie, the State of North Carolina comes in with their auditor. They audit the books. They pull up every dime you spent and give back a percentage of what you paid in in taxes. What you paid in, to keep the movie business here, they'll give you a percentage of that back. It's an incentive to keep the movies here. They put in that governor we had up there and he stopped it. When the time come to cough up the incentive money, they wouldn't give the movie people a damn thing. The state said, "We don't need you." So they had a meeting with the movie people and the movie people said, "Guess what? We made movies in California before you people were ever born. We'll take our apples and go home." That's the reason there's no more movies made here. I ain't done nothing. I ain't had nothing to do. Since they outlawed everything out of North Carolina, nobody even knows your phone number anymore.

Be that as it may, Neil Castles continues to work in the movie industry into his 80s in different capacities. As a picture car finder there may be none better. It appears a lot of people still have Neil's phone number and use it regularly.

Nine

Taking on the Giant

In the late '80s and early '90s, Neil and Jean were enjoying a wonderful life with their family and friends while owning and operating a marina near their home in Charlotte. Neil was making movies and Jean was running the marina. Some pretty famous people frequented the marina, which sold much more than just gas.

I was working in a movie job and a boy told me the old man that owned a marina was going to sell it. I said, "Well, I'd love to have that. That would give me something to make money the rest of my life." So I went up there and bought it. Castles Pit Stop Marina was on Lake Norman and I give it to Jean and she managed it and run it. It had two gas pumps, high test and regular, that went down to the boat dock and you could gas your boat at the boat dock. The gas company come and filled them thousand-gallon tanks every two weeks or whenever we needed it. And you could pull your truck and fill it up too if you wanted to. We sold guns, ammunition, all kinds of fishing equipment, and Jean's a licensed firearms dealer now. She's got the book where every time you bought ammunition you had to sign and Earnhardt used to buy all the hunting ammunition and everything at the marina and filled up his boats there two or three times a week. That's Dale, Sr., not Dale, Jr. Him and Neil Bonnett come in there all the time fishing and buying whatever they wanted. He was always in and out of the marina every day or two and we'd talk and carry on. We talked about hunting and fishing all the time. Me and Chocolate Myers, his gasman, were always dealing with Dale. Every time we'd get ready to start a race Dale would stick his finger out the window at me and say, "You behave today." Me and him joked together. I dealt with his daddy a lot of times. Ralph raced all them dirt tracks everywhere and I knew him from going to those. When Dale came along, Ralph used to be at the racetrack with him and we'd sit around and talk. They had their lives and we had ours and we went our own way every day.

Nine. Taking on the Giant

Castles Pit Stop Marina on Lake Norman, North Carolina, was a popular spot for boaters, fishermen, and hunters like Dale Earnhardt and Neil Bonnett (Neil Castles Family Collection).

Trouble reared its ugly head when Neil and Jean had their first brush with environmental problems. It was the tip of the iceberg as similar difficulties would plague the Castles' lives in some form for decades, literally for the rest of their lives.

The environmental people were looking at fuel tanks back then and I didn't know anything about it. Well, the fuel company had put them tanks in the ground for Joe Worsham that owned the marina. They had serviced them for him from the time they were put in.

After we bought the marina this dude comes over to Jean and says, "I'm going to have to turn your gas off and take the pumps out." I was out of town working on a movie. He said, "I'll tell you what I'll do. I'll do you a favor. I'll sell you the pumps and the tanks for a dollar and you sign this release that you're responsible for any spillage that's been there." Well, he got Jean to sign the damn thing for a dollar. Then he come back the next week saying he was going to take the damn tanks out because they weren't sure that they still wouldn't be held responsible for it.

When I got involved, Jean had taken full responsibility for every bit of contamination there. The people running those tanks had been running them over and spilling fuel for years. From up there where the tanks were in the ground all the way down the hill to the pumps at the dock all that land was saturated in fuel. I had the environmental people tell me it was going to cost me more to clean that up. "You'll have to dig up Lake Norman to stop that shit." That's when I said it was time to get rid of this mess. I had some people I was talking to about taking over a race team and found a building up there in Paw Creek that was empty and for sale. I called the real estate people and they came and showed it to us.

Incredibly, Neil sold one contaminated piece of land and bought another one.

We sold the marina and moved from the marina down here. There was a salesman with a real estate company and I was looking for a building that was big enough to house the cars and equipment I had. I bought a building from Exxon and didn't do a big investigation. Jean and I just came down here and looked at it. This was right up here at Paw Creek across from the Exxon tank farm. We called it Castles Auto and Truck Services, Inc. Right after we bought it, the lady across the street from where we bought said she had gas in her drinking water and it was contaminated.

So here comes all these investigators in to investigate it. They said the gas came from the building we bought and we had contaminated her water. I went to some environmentalists and they started doing soil testing on our property. Every time they took samples, I took samples and was gathering up information. They decided that there was a huge spill. They thought that when Exxon owned the building they didn't know what they had over there. It was where Exxon had fixed all their fuel trucks from the airport. Everything at the airport went through there to be repaired.

The battle begins over just whose contamination it was. The obvious and reasonable is not so clear-cut when you are opposing a corporate giant with bottomless pockets.

We got in a big fight with Exxon over the contamination. Exxon said it was ours. I said it was theirs. I had just bought the building. They said that when we bought it, we took responsibility for it. Well, we went back and forth

Nine. Taking on the Giant

Castles Auto and Truck Services, Inc., in Paw Creek, North Carolina, was ultimately supposed to house Neil Castles' future racing operations. It turned into a battleground circa 1992 (Neil Castles Family Collection).

with Exxon battling over that gas. Finally we made them cut the side out of tank number three in front of the building and had them go in and inspect the bottom of the tank. Well, when they took a hole in the side of the tank, they found three hundred and something holes in the bottom bigger than a baseball. And they had been running a water bottom on it for years. See, as long as you've got water underneath it, it'll raise the gas. They'd run a water bottom on it for 20 years, we found out after we got into the records. The gas stayed on top of the water. All the gas and water and them baseball holes eat that bottom up. There wasn't a bottom down there, but rust. There's still probably 30 of them up there now. They're tearing them down and building them back right now.

Exxon exports the problem.

Well, we went toe to toe with them. I started checking on what they were hauling off. They were digging up that contaminated soil from around those tanks and carrying it over to a landfill on Oakdale Road about 12 miles away and dumping it and it soaked in gas. I followed the trucks over there and got jars of dirt and gas and took it to the lab. That brought in that the landfill was full of gas that Exxon had sent over there. I had pictures of me driving the car, going in there, and taking the samples. I had a man in the back seat with a movie camera. I got probably 100,000 feet of film. They didn't solve the problem, they just spread it out.

Enter the suits. Lots of them.

They kept battling with me and we had discovery. I had 27 lawyers from Exxon on my front porch right here saying that I had contaminated the whole end of town. They were going to do testing on that property. They started drilling and monitoring wells and testing and all of this and they brought pages, hundreds of pages, of discovery for us to answer. Well, I answered some of it and we went into deposition. Well, my deposition is about a foot thick. They kept running into more money than I could afford and the lawyers kept running up the bill higher and higher. So Jean and I went to Washington and hired two law firms and they come down here.

The contaminated office of the Paw Creek Environmental Association in Paw Creek, North Carolina, which was ground zero in the battle with Exxon circa 1992 (Neil Castles Family Collection).

Nine. Taking on the Giant

Neil swings into action with hundreds of others involved. He was fighting Exxon attorneys with DC attorneys and enlisted the assistance of others with the same problems as he and Jean. But perhaps his strongest ally was yet to come.

Now, the house next to the building we bought was a nice house that they built for the terminal manager. I put an office in that house and called it Paw Creek Environmental Investigations and put in a conference table with 12 chairs around it. We covered the walls with all the stuff environmentally we'd found. How much Exxon had damaged and where they were doing it. We set up a committee. We drug in all the people in this end of town that had gas in their water being forced to buy city water on account of that contamination. So we set up memberships and had a huge amount of people that were a part of Paw Creek Environmental Association.

In the meantime, I got the newspaper involved in it. The *Charlotte Observer*. Public opinion. I got WBT-TV in it. Mike Cozza was the head reporter for WBT-TV and Bob Inman was his boss. They followed the case everywhere it went from beginning to end. They stayed on top of this thing with us and no matter what happened. If we went to Raleigh, Mike Cozza went to Raleigh. I'll bet I've got thousands of feet of tape with me and him and Jean going up and down the road to the offices and courthouses. They kind of lost their jobs on account of this thing. The network didn't think they should have been putting so much effort into it because of Exxon. It looked kind of like they stepped on Exxon's toes. I think Exxon got them both fired, but I don't know that. Anyhow, Bob Inman bought himself a house in the mountains and started writing. One of the books he wrote was *Home Fires Burning*. It was a movie, too. We made it in Wilmington. He's still writing books every day. They put Mike Cozza in charge of a park across town. I haven't heard anything from Mike in a long time. I don't know how he's doing.

Now it was time to introduce the fight to the judicial system. Surely justice would be swift and fair.

We took it to federal court in downtown Charlotte about 1995, blaming Exxon for the contamination, and presented our samples of what we had. It was a jury trial and that jury went on for a week or two. The federal judge when it was over with said, "Well, I'm not happy with this. I'm going to tell you what I'm going to do. I'm going to throw this case out of my court. I'm not going to award anybody a winner or loser. I'm throwing it out." He wasn't going to rule on it because we won the case.

We went straight to the Court of Appeals in Richmond. The court ruled on it and ruled in our favor. We won the case in Richmond, Virginia, with the federal government. When we won it, before we got home Exxon appealed it. Exxon appealed it to another court in Richmond. We went to three different courts in Richmond. Well, we won all three trips up there and they awarded us the case. They said that it was Exxon's contamination and they were responsible for it years before they ever got caught with it. They told Exxon to pay the people what they owed them or settle with them. Whatever it takes.

Exxon appealed it to the Court of Appeals in Washington, D.C. So we had two of the biggest law firms in Washington, D.C., standing at the door. They brought in truckloads of stuff. It took a bus to carry all the documents into the courthouse every day. The Court of Appeals in Washington, D.C., looked at the case and said, "This case is cut and dried. Exxon, it was your gas, you left it there, you're responsible. Pay the people and drop it." We had too much evidence. So they wrote us a check for several hundred thousand dollars. We sued them for $2 million and I think we got most of it. It was like a class action lawsuit and we won it hands down.

The lawsuit was over, or was it? And all the residents of the Paw Creek Community were happy, or were they? More lawsuits followed.

Everybody in the committee was in the court downtown over the contamination. Bob Cloninger, who used to work for the railroad, was in the office with Jean, and they handled the committee's stuff. The whole walls in that office were lined with people's names with how much cancer they had, all the doctors' reports, and everything. It spread out. Everybody's wells were contaminated. Their land was contaminated. Therefore, they had contaminated property they couldn't sell. There was a lot of people going to lose a lot of property. So there was a lot of angry people and being as Bob was in charge, they shot at him a couple of times. The lawsuit had brought on all this contaminated property. I don't think Exxon gave a shit about shooting at anybody. They had all the people from Raleigh coming in there every day wanting information. So Raleigh had to get involved. With WBT-TV following me everywhere I went, it stayed on the news 24 hours a day and night. In the meantime, I didn't have any more money, so I had to go to work. I had

Nine. Taking on the Giant

to pay them lawyers so they got most of it. I went to Wilmington, got me a job with the movie company, and went to work.

It really was not over at all. Exxon still intended to pursue the matter, not willing to give up or pay up any more, so an Exxon mediator was sent in to bring about a conclusion.

They brought in some damn mediator from Texas and his wife. They rented him a house in Kannapolis completely furnished, furnished him a car, and he come here. He sat right there in that den with me and Jean and said he was here to settle the differences between Castles Auto and Truck Services, Paw Creek Environmental, Exxon, and us. He was a mediator and his wife was a lawyer and she was a mediator and we talked a little bit and he wanted to know what it would take to satisfy me. I said, "Well, I might be hard to handle." I wasn't committing to nothing because I don't know who this damn guy is. They called me and Jean to go over to his house over in Kannapolis and we met with him and his wife and had coffee. He got involved with our Washington lawyers. We had two law firms in Washington, D.C., that were working for us. All the Washington lawyers had to go through a North Carolina lawyer. Mr. Gaskins, an Exxon lawyer, was still putting demands on me and Jean with his people.

It was discovery. Instead of writing a letter, an Exxon guy come out to our house with this mediator and he wanted to go through our house and any documents that he could find he wanted to take with him. He wanted to examine our furniture. He wanted to examine our closets and see what was the quality of clothes we were wearing. He wanted to drill a well in our yard to see if the water was contaminated. He was going to check our furniture to see who made it and if that could have contaminated the house itself. That bedroom suite in there was made in California and shipped here. He traced it back to where it was made out of wilmidge chestnut in Los Angeles by a major manufacturer and shipped here. It was not manufactured in Charlotte and had no environmental impact. It was very high-priced wood and cost a fortune to get it. He was like a rabbit in a field. He said, "I'll have to get with Mr. Gaskins and see just what time he wants to be here." I said, "Well, I don't know that I want to see Mr. Gaskins." "We have got to inform him that we're going to be present while he does his investigation between you and your wife and the Paw Creek Committee."

The next day he showed up and said, "We've decided in the morning we're going to bring Mr. Gaskins over and let him do his examination at about eight o'clock." I said, "I don't think so." He said, "What do you mean 'I don't think so'?" I said, "You see that coffee table setting there?" He said, "Yes." I said, "There's a .44 magnum laying on that table with six shells in it. One of them is steel-jacketed and will blow the damn engine block in two and he won't drive his car no more." I said, "The second one is a hollow point and I can blow his damn leg off and he'll stop walking. The third one is a steel-jacketed that I can blow his head off with. The fourth one I'm going to save for your ass." He said, "Now wait just a minute." I said, "You go get Mr. Gaskins and I'll be sitting here in this chair tomorrow morning at eight o'clock waiting on you bastards to show up."

The next morning [at] six-thirty he showed up on the porch ringing the doorbell. We come in the den and sat down and I said, "What's the deal? What time's he going to be here?" He said, "He won't be here today. We've had a change of plans. Exxon has decided that they would like to withdraw all complaints they have against Castles and Castles' Committee. They're dropping it right there. It will go no further. They will not be involved with the Castles any further." I told the mediator I'd kill that son of a bitch so bring him on. That was the direct information from the mediator from Houston, Texas. That ended it right there.

The lawsuit was over. The case was won. But there is a post script. Exxon fired Mr. Gaskins. He became the river keeper on the Catawba River at Lake Wylie. He worked at that for a while and then he went to Houston to mediate on another case. He was involved in a wreck where somebody got killed and he liked to got killed himself. I never seen him for a long time and we were coming out of Home Depot one time and somebody brushed my shirt sleeve and I turned around and it was him. He looked at me and took off out the door. That's the last time I ever seen him. He's still here in town. He's still a well-known environmental lawyer.

By 1995 Castles Auto and Truck Services, Inc., versus Exxon Corporation was over. Neil heaps praise on his attorneys for their handling of the lawsuit. One of the D.C. firms was Millstein, Cohen, Hausfield, and Toll. They had squared off against Exxon previously when they won a $5,000,000,000 judgment for the residents of Prince William Sound, Alaska. Does the Exxon Valdeze ring a bell?

Most unfortunately, though, the real horror was yet to come.

Nine. Taking on the Giant

I have a map of the Paw Creek neighborhood and I put a black dot on it everywhere somebody got sick. The map is covered with black dots. The map is covered with cancer. They told me that I breathed enough fumes out of that building to have stage four lung cancer and that went to my eye. It had a spot on that bone behind my left eye. They weren't supposed to take my eye. They were supposed to do something with that spot on the bone. But this doctor and another were only in it for the money and they must have taken 50 old peoples' eyes out just to get the money to open another new medical building. They were supposed to put me back a glass eye, an artificial eye, and fix my face. We had a plastic surgeon and all of that paid for and then they refused to do it. They said they didn't think I would be here long enough for it to be worthwhile.

So I got involved with the cancer doctor here in town and every 28 days I took chemo at Presbyterian Hospital. They did it every 28 days for several months and Doc Taylor said, "Neil, I'll tell you what. Go back over there to the hospital and see this doctor who's in charge of radiation. I think if we put radiation on top of this chemo we can kill it." So I went back over there and started on radiation. They gave me radiation every day for a year.

With his left eye removed and part of his skull cut away, Neil was told it was not worth the time and effort it would take to reconstruct his face. The medical experts did not think he would live that long anyway, so they just stretched his skin across the vacant eye socket and sent him on his way. They obviously did not know who they were dealing with: a man who had spent a lifetime staring down Death regularly as a champion stock car driver and a Hollywood stunt man. Now Neil just stares it down with one eye.

Finally, they found a spot on my lungs and we radiated that. They found one more spot on my lung they couldn't do nothing with. The doctor said, "Neil, the only thing, we're scared to try to biopsy it. I can do one thing. I can cut you right across your shoulder blade, go down between your lungs and your ribs, and I'll take a chunk of that lung off." I said, "When do you want to do it?" He said, "Whenever you do." I said, "How about eight o' clock in the morning?" I went to the hospital and they cut me across my back and took that whole lobe off that lung. When they took it out there was no more sign of cancer in my lungs or nothing else.

Still I'm doing my radiation and all that. I have to have a cat scan and MRI every 30 days. So they found a spot in my head. They said I had a tumor in my head. They said I had a brain tumor. Then all the doctors came out of the woodwork. I've got a brain tumor and I'm going to die. This was about two years ago. This doctor said, "Well, Neil, we can't biopsy it because we can't hit it with a needle and we can't hit it with radiation. If we do anything with it, it's going to spread everywhere. The only thing we've got to do is drill a hole in your head down there and go in and see what's there." I said, "I'll be there in the morning."

I went over there the next day to the hospital and they put me in surgery, the operating room, and drilled a hole in my head down through my skull. They took a sample out and didn't like what they found and sent it to the lab. So all the lab people at Presbyterian Hospital come down there and took a sample out of my head. These other doctors that's been fighting back and forth to protect the oil companies and everybody else come and got them a handful of samples out of my head from a brain tumor. I stayed in the hospital a week, got out, and come home. The doctors took Jean and Neil, Jr., into a back room and said, "We didn't get anything out of his head to tell us anything. The only thing we found in Neil's head looked like a big blob of snot. Neil, Jr., got up in the middle of the meeting and said, "What did you find?" "We found nothing. Out of all the lab tests you had nothing in your head except something that looked like a big blob of snot."

Is the ordeal finally over, or is it?

Jean didn't have any problems at all. We just had the office and building in Paw Creek by

During an interview session on February 8, 2018, Neil Castles at 83 years old strikes a casual pose which much belies the fearless racer, stunt man, and ecological crusader that still lives within (Perry Allen Wood Racing Archives).

the tank farm. There was a neighborhood there, but we were living here at Pine Island Country Club and at the farm we bought. Later I carried a gallon jar full of that dirt and gas down there to the Charlotte City Council and set it on the table. I took the lid off and they called the fire department. Everything with Exxon is over. The State of North Carolina is still harassing me about it. I want to thank Allen Brotherton and Eddie Knox who are local attorneys that helped us through this legal thing with Exxon. People that went through all that with you, you need to say thanks to.

Neil is 83 years old as he relates his story with his loving wife Jean by his side in their beautiful living room with the golf course out the window in the background. And he is not done yet.

Ten

Heading for the Checkered Flag

These days in his ninth decade, Neil Castles stays plenty busy. There are demands on him from old-time racing organizations to show up for their events. The movie makers still depend on Neil to supply that car or cars to lend authenticity to projects for screens both big and small. Having downsized to about two acres of beautiful babbling brookside living along the par four 18th fairway of the Pine Island Country Club, Neil and Jean take care of each other and their property.

Every morning when I get up I've got two acres of trees and yard work to do. And I'm always hunting different cars for different people. I've still got a lot of people that like to rent cars if they know who to rent them to. I've got a 40-foot trailer just stacked with racing stuff. I've got a car trailer with a '73 Dodge Charger in it that's pretty well complete. Not a racecar, just a Charger. We used it in a movie. There was a Bojangles commercial where they had a Dukes of Hazzard car painted up with a chicken on top of it and it jumped a police car. I've still got that car. I sold the police car to some taxi driver. I've got one racecar, a Camaro that we built for Jean's brother Dennis Gallion to run at Hickory Speedway. It won four championships in a row. I got the Junior Johnson car out of a bank building in North Wilkesboro and brought it down to Hickory and made a commercial with the two of them.

One question bears asking. What if Exxon had never entered into the Castles' lives? How does he think things might have been without his contaminated acres in Paw Creek?

I would have bought that building with full intentions of operating my own race shop and team without having to be obligated to everybody in the world. I had a doctor that wanted to sponsor a lot of it. I was working towards a lot of things to get a sponsorship to go racing. And I had talked very close

Ten. Heading for the Checkered Flag

to Chrysler. But I didn't want to jump on Cotton's feet or nobody else's that had been very good to me. The Pettys was another one. I had in mind that Dale Sr., would probably have wanted me to see what I could do with Dale Jr. He was coming along as a teenager by then around 1990 and showing signs of wanting to be a racer, too. I would have helped wherever I could if asked. He made it OK. And I guess my health would be a little better.

Yes, it can be said that Dale Earnhardt, Jr., did OK as one of the most popular drivers in stock car racing history. Recently he moved on to another career as a broadcaster and will succeed there as well.

And naturally, many of the brave racing pioneers of the '40s and '50s and those who followed have moved on as well. One by one his old racing and movie pals are leaving him, and Neil knew everybody.

I stayed close friends with Buck Baker the rest of his life. He had that driving school at the speedway and I'd stop by and we'd talk old times. Buck was good to me, taught me a lot, and gave me a lot of work, especially in those Chryslers. He had one of those chairs that raised and helped you stand up. Even Buddy Baker is gone now.

Buck Baker left us in 2002, Cotton Owens and Andy Griffith in 2012, Buddy Baker in 2015, and on and on it goes. Once Neil called on a friend and got the sad news the hard way.

Larry died not too long ago. I called his house to talk to him and his wife said, "This is not exactly funny." I said, "What do you mean?" She said, "He ain't here no more." We were always talking. I never knew he was sick. We were all like family. Larry Frank was part of the family.

Another of Neil's best and oldest friends was perennial independent Elmo Langley. When Elmo finally won his first Grand National race in Spartanburg in 1966, it was Neil in second place right behind him.

Me and Elmo talked at Rockingham when he was driving the pace car. Me and him were talking about old times and he was going to Japan for that stock car race and I said, "Well, I don't think I'm going to catch that boat." That was the last meeting I ever had with Elmo Langley before he died. We was good friends. They put Elmo in somebody's Ford down there in Texas

Neil "Soapy" Castles

to outrun me in 1972 for that championship. They were determined to get me out of the point lead if they could get Elmo to outrun me in that Ford. I ran with him all day and we battled back and forth and got down to the end of the race and I blew his doors off and went on. He was supposed to beat me and didn't get it done.

Elmo and Bill Champion were always playing games with each other. Elmo was on the second floor of a motel down in Georgia one time and Champ come out of the motel room. So Elmo dropped a watermelon and it barely missed his shoulder and if it had hit him in the head it would have killed him. But there's a picture of me and Elmo at that meeting in Rockingham and I never saw him again. In a month he was gone.

The Rockingham meeting between Neil and Elmo was October 20, 1996. On November 21, 1996, Elmo Langley passed away while driving the pace car around the Suzuka Circuitland in Suzuka City, Japan. Buddy Baker, an

Pace car driver Elmo Langley behind the wheel is arm-in-arm with his old pal Neil Castles on race day, October 20, 1996. That date is visible on the car door at the North Carolina Motor Speedway in Rockingham. A month and a day later, Elmo passed away driving a pace car in Suzuka City, Japan (Neil Castles Family Collection).

Ten. Heading for the Checkered Flag

announcer working the television broadcast for the Nashville Network, was his passenger and quickly switched off the car and brought it to a stop.

As the writing of this book was winding down, a horrible tragedy took place in the early morning hours of April 28, 2018, on I-85 near Carnesville, Georgia. A legendary racer for the ages, James Harvey Hylton and his son, James Harvey Hylton, Jr., known as Tweety, were killed in the crash of their truck pulling the enclosed trailer with their ARCA car inside. Neil and James had a very special relationship and he wanted to share it here.

When Hylton first started running, we were running that racecourse at the back end of Long Island, Bridgehampton. That was the first time I was in an old Dodge. He had a Dodge, and Chrysler had give him a lot of springs and torsion bars and stuff. When the race was over he said, "I got the floor of my shop full of that old Dodge stuff. Bring your truck to my shop on Monday morning and you can load it up. I want it out of my way." So he give me all the old Dodge stuff he had. I appreciated it because I didn't have nothing.

Many years later, Neil found himself in a position to help James and this was serious.

Every time I did a movie, he wanted a job. He wanted to put his car in it. See, I could put the car on rental. We were in Atlanta to do the movie *Six Pack*. He called me and said, "I want to talk to you. I need a job bad." I said, "Well, I'm at the Holiday Inn at Powers Ferry." I give him the room number and said, "Knock on that door with a cup of coffee before six o'clock in the morning and we'll talk." He was out there banging on the door the next morning. "I'll put you to work on this show because I'm in charge of all the picture cars. I can put you to work as one of my picture car helpers, drivers, and get you on the payroll. Once you get on the payroll, I'll move you from one spot to another where I need you to keep you employed for more than a short amount of time." I put him on the show and kept him in my motel room ten days. I had a big motel room.

Well, the weather was bad as hell. I mean cold and wet. He come up there and says, "I got a problem. Evelyn is sick and that young'un is going to die if we don't get a doctor." "Where they at?" "We were staying over yonder at that motel, but there ain't no place to eat or nothing." I said, "Where's Evelyn and the boy?" He had an old box truck. "They're in the back of the truck." I said, "Let's go see what's going on." I opened the back door and said,

"Evelyn, are you sick?" She couldn't even hold her head up. "Just sit right there. I'll be back in a minute."

Hell, I went straight to the field hospital and got me a nurse. I brought the nurse down there and said, "Check these two and see if they got pneumonia or what the hell they got." He was afraid if they had the flu, it would spread and he'd lose his job. I said, "Don't worry about the job. You work for me." He'd worked for me three or four days before he ever told me they were sick. The nurse checked them and went back to the field hospital and got the doctor. Well, he come down there and said we've only got two ambulances for this whole racetrack and we can't let them go. James said, "I got a car, but I don't know where to go." Doctor said, "Here's the address. Take them to the hospital and the doctor will be waiting on you." They put them in the hospital four or five days, treated them, got them well, and he was always grateful because I put him on the payroll of every show I done. I had him on the payroll on *Greased Lightning* driving one of the dirt cars.

It has been repeated so many times, but racing was a family in those days. It is not like that now. Everybody had each other's back. Neil and James would have done anything for each other. He told us the Marty Robbins bull story earlier. And now another of his comrades is gone, as is the little boy Tweety, who was so sick in the back of the box truck. Evelyn moves ahead without her ex-husband and son. Neil, Jean, and all the Castles hurt badly for them.

Neil Castles has a lot to be proud of and his family has loved and supported him through thick and thin and there has been a lot of both.

We have three children. Susan is the oldest, born in the fifties, because I was running my '56 Ford then. She was a neonatal nurse in Charleston for a while. She moved from Charleston to Wilmington because they live in Wilmington and she was tired of running up and down the road. Her husband Ken is a real estate broker. He is second to the head of all real estate bought, sold, or traded on Bald Head Island. Susan's got three boys, Taylor, Robert, and Jesse.

Donna is an accountant for a major construction company in Houston, Texas. Her husband Dean is involved with removing and installing valves for the nuclear plants.

Neil Castles, Jr., has twins, Zac and Chloe, and calls Wilmington home, but is on the road mostly these days due to the film industry leaving North Carolina. I was working on *Matlock*. I had to have two T-Model police cars

Ten. Heading for the Checkered Flag

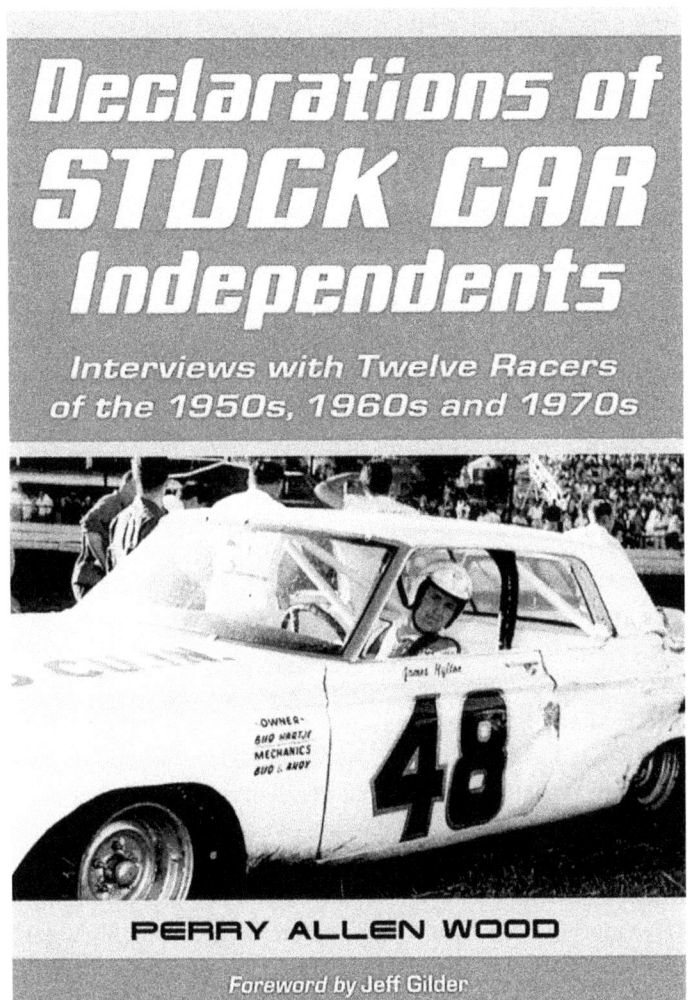

Neil's close friend James Hylton and his son Tweety were killed in a traffic accident on April 18, 2018. James was honored with the cover and final chapter of McFarland's *Declarations of Stock Car Independents* in 2010 (Perry Allen Wood Racing Archives).

and I dressed him up and made a police [officer] out of him and put him in a T-Model.

Another time they were doing a thing on the Second World War draft to sign up new soldiers. We had to have an Army halftrack and I found one. I got a hold of the transportation coordinator and made arrangements that

Neil "Soapy" Castles

if we could crank it up we could use it. So me and Neil went over there all day one Saturday, charged the batteries on it, and got it running. I drove it around a cotton patch down there right out of Wilmington, showed Neil how to drive it, and two days later he was driving it in a parade around the courthouse in that town.

Neil Castles, Jr., is in his prime in the movie industry with some acting roles as well as being transportation coordinator. As of this writing he is filming of Son of Shaft *in Atlanta. He is involved in all kinds of shows. Big shows and little ones. The children and grandchildren of Jean and Neil Castles can be assured in knowing that their parents and grandparents are tempered strong as steel to have experienced all the good times and bad times of eight decades. As they lead their own lives spread across the land, the Castles are a strong family still staying close and supporting each other.*

If anybody in the world could ever roll with the punches and adapt to whatever happens, Neil is no doubt a champion at that, too. Recently, his loving Jean has presented a special situation that Neil is taking a day, an hour, and a minute at a time.

Jean's in that Alzheimer's program at Duke University. They recommended to get her a baby to take care of to keep her mind on what she was doing. I've adapted to the situation. He looks good sitting up on the table at the Chick-fil-A eating chicken. So all of them women in that Alzheimer's program have now got a baby to take care of. I guess they know what they're doing. It's been a slight change of plans, but we're getting by with it. I'm not taking her to a nursing home. I'm taking care of her. Her grandmother died with it. Her mother died with it. Two sisters died with it. She's got an aunt right now in Morganton with three cousins that's all got it. It's all inherited.

I've started a little notebook about some of her favorite places. I've got a picture of her sitting in a chair on the waterfront in Newport, Rhode Island. That's her favorite chair and that's where she wants to sit. There won't be no nursing home. I'm taking care of her just as I always have. We've always been there for each and nothing has changed. Anyway, I've been keeping all the loose ends tied up. I always will.

Jean Castles traveled with Neil to all those dusty, dimly lit dirt tracks for so very many years. She was there rooting for him and supporting him through the wins and losses, the finishes and crashes, the injuries and the deaths, and the

Ten. Heading for the Checkered Flag

hilarious and the desperate. She shared in the glory of the victories and championship standing proudly by his side all the way no matter what. If Neil did it, Jean did it, too. Whatever Neil faced, Jean dealt with at the same time, only there was a slight twist. She was primarily the one raising the kids. Neil never ever once mentioned that she was not supportive of him or even hinted for him to quit risking his life either before a roaring crowd or whirring camera. Now Neil is faced with the challenge of meeting a new set of special needs and he is up to the task. Jean helped Neil fight the ravages of ground contamination to his body. She was too tough to lose that fight. All those people around Paw Creek got sick decades ago, but not Jean. Now the adversary is heredity, which may be the most formidable foe of there is. But Neil and the whole family have got this. It will be all right.

Meanwhile, Neil has plenty of other routines to keep him busy. For one, he still has fans.

My mailbox stays full, too. When Susan comes home she starts opening the envelopes, saying, "Daddy sign this, Daddy sign that." She licks them and

Three veterans of old-time racing festivals and autograph sessions are, from left to right, Neil Castles, Perry Allen Wood, and Tiger Tom Pistone, seen here at Alex Beam's Memory Lane Museum in Mooresville, North Carolina, on May 17, 2015 (Perry Allen Wood Racing Archives).

sends them back. People buy pictures off the Internet. I don't know what they pay for them, but they buy them off the Internet. And they always want something else autographed. All I ask for is a stamped envelope with a return address on it. I'll sign it and put it in the mail to you.

There is one expertise for which it appears Neil Castles will always be on constant call. Movie people know where to go.

I get a phone call and some movie somewhere needs a car that is impossible to locate. But I've got a list of people that have any kind of old car in the world. I hunt for everything. I've also got a list of where all these old buses are and where we can get them. Up until Harold Russell died, he had as many cars as Alex Beam has. He lived in Gastonia, North Carolina, and was a collector. I used a lot of his cars. When I was working in Wilmington and needed a '40 Ford convertible, I'd call Harold and he'd say, "They'll be one there in the morning." Warren Betters used to call me to get the cars for anything that was going to be made on the East Coast and tell me what we're going to do and what we're going to blow up.

Neil Castles tries to reflect on his life that is actually three or four lives in one. For some reason it is hard for him to do. His accomplishments are many and his regrets very few. Maybe he would have stayed away from England and Paw Creek if he could do it all over again.

I guess I was most proud to win that championship. It was touch and go with a lot of people trying to stop me from doing it. Me and Richard Petty won the two NASCAR stock car championships that year in 1972. I've had so many people help me and encourage me along the way. The work ethic of my grandparents and mother and father taught me early on that life was tough and no nobody was going to hand me anything I didn't earn. Of course Buddy Shuman and William Thompson got me to racing and Buddy gave me a name I'm still called today. I owe so much to so many in racing that it's impossible to name them all. The Colvins and even Bill France influenced me along the way. How could I leave out maybe the biggest of all, Richard Howard? It's the same in the movie business with people like Everett Creach, and Carey Loftin that helped me perfect my stunting skills. Producers, directors, actors, and the men and women behind the scenes that guided me through a new and unknown job that's still pretty much where I am now, finding picture cars. The movie business

Ten. Heading for the Checkered Flag

was good to me and I tried to be good to the movie business until they sent me out in the street.

There is another group that is the most important of all. They came along one at a time, but are all together now and fully involved. They will always be with Neil and Jean through whatever comes their way.

Jean has been with me for over 60 years through whatever racing, the movies, and the big oil company could throw at me. At us! She always supported me and never once did she tell me to give something up. Never was something too dangerous or too this or too that. Not that she didn't show her concern, she just stood by me and was for me. She took good care of me and now it's my turn to take good care of her. I'm not going anywhere, not for a while yet anyway. We vowed "for better or worse" and that's how it's always been and will continue to be.

On April 26, 2018, Neil displays the original Fireball Roberts helmet, reassembled by Jean from pieces, and the Joe Eubanks gift helmet Neil used in West Memphis, Arkansas, on August 14, 1955 (Perry Allen Wood Racing Archives).

As for the kids, Susan, Donna, and Neil, Jr., are all set with their own families to look after in different parts of the country. Me and Jean got them started and saw them make it on their own. They'll always be with us to help us get through whatever is ahead. Most big holidays we figure out how to get together and have a good old time. I couldn't have done it without all my family's advice, support, and most of all, love. That's the strongest thing we've got going for us. It's really all we need.

The Castles family in 2012 with, from left to right, Donna, Neil Jr., Jean, Neil Sr., and Susan (Susan Castles Collection).

Henry Neil "Soapy" Castles has had so much for which to be thankful. He has a lot of laps left in his life's race and he has a faithful crew to get him to the checkered flag. He is a pioneer and a survivor. He is absolutely as tough as they come. It took a lot of fearlessness and grit to get him this far because he has the face of courage.

Eleven

Neil's Children Reflect

Susan Elizabeth Castles

Susan is 60 years old and lives in Wrightsville Beach, North Carolina, with her husband Ken Mowbray. She has three sons. After a long career as a neonatal intensive care nurse, she now works in film as a set nurse.

Although my father is best known for his history in NASCAR, it by no means defines who he is. Unlike many of the sport's earlier legends, when the time came to get out of the driver's seat, he didn't continue in the organization in another capacity. His life took him down many different and unexpected paths; some were opportunities while others were obstacles. That may be true in all our lives, but one of the things I admire most about him is his ability to fearlessly accept a challenge. He took his abilities, his God-given gifts, and used them to conquer whatever landed in front of him. He is a true athlete, both physically and mentally, with extraordinary strength and stamina. He created a second career in the film industry that took him far beyond retirement age. He beat cancer. He beat Exxon. He became a champion for the environment. He's the man in his 80s standing on his roof with a leaf blower cleaning out the gutters. A conqueror. He won't take no for an answer and he never gives up. He has been a warrior, but he also has a softer side. His love and devotion to my mother, and hers to him, is what inspires me most. I hope that others will see him as I do: an example of courage, strength, selflessness, and love.

Donna Jean Wolfer

Donna Jean Wolfer is 57 years old, an accountant, and lives with her husband Dean in Spring, Texas. They have four children and 8 grandchildren.

Neil "Soapy" Castles

According to history, the name Castles has been around since 1102. Legend says in the old days, when someone distinguished himself as being brave, honorable, and possessing utmost integrity, he was awarded the last name Castles. People knew they had met someone they could depend on and they would honor their word. I was fortunate to be born to one of those individuals. If my parents said they were going to do something, they did it. Our parents were stern, taught us manners, to be trustworthy, stand up for yourself and your family, don't take crap from anyone, fight for what you believe in, and to love God. Work ethic was taught at an early age and they both showed us by example. These are the lessons in life that would stay with each one of us and see us through the good and not so good stages of our lives.

Growing up in a racing family was never like our friends' families. We had our normal life and then we had our weekend life and family at the tracks. Dad was very protective of us girls when we were young, doing his best to protect us from the infield's colorful attractions going on every Sunday. Some of my fondest memories of my dad's life in racing were spent on Sundays in the fenced in area for the families. There the lines of motorhomes backed up to the fence, and from the numerous cars you could eat like a king. Everyone had food, and I mean lots of food. My mother was no exception as she could feed an army. Oh, but when Wendell Scott's family drove up and popped that trunk you were in for a treat if you got a piece of Ms. Mary's fried chicken.

This was our weekend family. Some of the best naps I ever had were to the hum of 40 racecars. This was a life we were born into. However, it was not all fun. Growing up in the world of racing you lived with the fear that when your father left for the track he might not return. I can count on one hand the times I have seen Dad cry; one of them was the day Tiny Lund was killed.

The life of racing follows you everywhere. I can't recall one time that we ever went out to eat that someone did not approach my dad. I always believed he must have known everyone, at least in every town we visited. My father has an unusual sense of humor, one that if you are not close to him you might not understand, but he always had this charismatic persona about him. People either liked him or they didn't, but what you saw is what you got and we love him.

Susan and I were fortunate that we were able to travel all over the USA with the racecar behind us. We were on the road from the time school was out till the week before school started, with just a few periods of being at home. I use to swear my dad could drive while he slept. I have stayed up many a night in the front seat of that truck talking to Dad to keep him awake so we could make it a little further down the road before he stopped and

Eleven. Neil's Children Reflect

slept. We didn't have planes or big semis back then; it was the car hauler, Winnebago, and a truck going all over the country. It was an adventure.

Holidays were always festive and full of family in our lives. Christmas was always a huge deal as it was the holiday that didn't have a race. Our tree was always live and cut down by Dad. The floor was covered in gifts, each one specially picked and wrapped. Websites today had nothing on our mother. She could bake, cook, and make anything you could imagine. Christmas candles were made from our old crayons melted down. Holly came straight from the tree outside, and the smells of our home during this time will stay with me forever. Dad loved every type of Christmas candy. There were bowls everywhere always full, and he still has that sweet tooth. Easters were always special, with white gloves and hats. Dad always presented us with an orchid corsage before church. It was a special time when the whole family could attend church together. With most Sundays spent at the track, it was important to Dad that God was not left out of our lives. We were fortunate that God was a daily part of our lives. Most people would not realize this about Dad, but he truly has a deep and strong relationship with our Lord and Savior.

As I look back at life I realize how lucky we were. We were not rich by any means, but Dad was a wonderful provider for his family. If there was a need he would always find a way to provide for it. I know that my siblings and I can agree that we were always well dressed and fed.

Our parents could not have raised three more polar opposite children, but they did a hell of a job. Susan is the mellow one, great at the violin, and a wonderful mother and nurse, and she is our voice of reason. Susan is a neonatal nurse with babies that fit in the palm of your hand and I have great admiration for my sister and her career. We all depend on Susan for medical direction.

Our late bloomer Neil Jr. (I was twelve when he was born) is the apple in everyone's eye. Neil Jr. is so much a blend of our parents. He has all of Dad's knowledge of cars, his mechanical mind, and can make something out of nothing. Following in Dad's footsteps into the movie industry, he has paved his own way and made his own name. Neil Jr. and my dad have a bond that most fathers and sons would envy; they can almost complete each other's sentences. Neil Jr. is also a wonderful provider for his children and I am so honored to call him my brother. When you look at Neil Jr. it is like seeing a live picture of our Grandfather Castles.

Then you get to me, the middle kid. I was the wild one and I look just like our mother. At the track they called me her shadow and now at the age of 57 it's uncanny how much I look like her, but ... I inherited my Dad's bull-in-a-china-shop personality. I liked fast cars and wasn't scared of anything. I loved my horses growing up and then I loved my Camaro. Life has taken me to many wonderful and exciting places, but now I live in Houston, Texas, where the good Lord blessed me with my husband Dean. I do accounting, which growing up was the furthest thing I ever dreamed of, but you know when God has plans for you, well, you follow. We have a large blended family with eight grandchildren. We have been blessed and have lived through tragedy, losing both our sons six years apart. Tragedy makes you realize all of those lessons our parents taught us are what gets you through. I am blessed to have my family with us each step of the way. My dad and my brother are our rocks, with Mom and Susan being the healing hands.

Now that we have reached the part of this family's journey where it is our time to assist our parents in their senior years, there is no one I would rather be doing this with than my sister and brother. We each bring an individual area to assist our parents and I think Dad would say we are doing OK. Dad asked me today, "How did all three of you end up this good?" We both responded at the same time, "God." In reflection, this family is not that abnormal. We never considered Dad famous; he is just our dad. He chose to race cars and do movies for a living. There is nothing glamorous about being hard-working. Our parents showed by example what Forever Love is. I can't recall a time that my dad ever left the house that he did not hug, kiss, and tell my mother he loved her. Even today all conversations between us end in "Love you." We have our ups and downs as all families do, but in the end the word is "family," and that is who and what Father and Mother raised.

In closing I just want to say, "Thank you, Dad and Mom for the ride. It has been an adventure." We love you and thank you for all of the lessons, all of the memories, which we will cherish forever.

Henry Neil Castles, Jr.

Neil Castles Jr. is the youngest of three kids and the only son. When not on the road, Neil calls Wilmington, North Carolina, home, which is where his children Zac and Chloe are in high school. Neil is currently a transportation coordinator for the film and television industry.

Neil "Soapy" Castles: who is this man to me? One word covers it all: "HERO"! He has been my father, my mentor, my best friend, but most of all

Eleven. Neil's Children Reflect

he has been my dad and as far as I'm concerned he's the best! To this day not one day goes by that I do not use something that my dad has taught me! He and I have raced Soap Box Derby cars together (yes, he started me from the ground up), as well as karts, and we were getting into limited late models when our plans were sidelined by our life-changing tangle with Exxon. God had a plan for us, though. That bump in the road called Exxon sent Dad and me fast-forward into the film and television industry, where we worked and lived together and I learned from the master of life lessons. My dad may not have graduated from high school, but he is one of the smartest men I know. There was never *not* a solution to a problem, and if we didn't have what we needed, we made it!

Every day of my life with my dad has been and continues to be a learning experience. Even on the few occasions we weren't working together, he was either talking to me in my mind or on the phone. I remember one night I had been up three days straight trying to prepare cars for a movie titled *My Life in Idlewild* and it was about three in the morning and I was dead tired trying to make a set of spark plug wires for a 1929 Studebaker and I couldn't for the life of me get the boots on the wires. Needless to say, anyone who has ever encountered my dad's temper will tell you I may have inherited a small amount of that from him. So I'm trying to get these spark plug boots on and it's like trying to push a rope. I'm getting mad and frustrated, so I put everything down walked outside with a Mountain Dew, hoping for some energy from the sugar, looking up at the night sky, and it hit me like a ton of bricks. I've seen Dad do this a hundred times. What's wrong with me? So I walked back in the shop, got a wire and boot, headed to the sink, opened the Gojo, stuck that wire in it, and slid it right in that boot like it was nothing. About ten minutes later I was done and headed home. I can recount a hundred more times that has happened and I'm sure it will as long as I live. Do I wish that Dad and I could have raced together for a living? Of course. I still have the burn in my gut as much as any racer, but God had a different plan for us and I don't regret a day!

In closing, I just want to thank you, Dad, for never missing a football game (or any event for that matter), for all the nights kart racing coming home dead tired while I slept (occasionally swerving in the road, beating my head against the window), and for being the best teacher that I ever had hands down and the best dad a boy could ask for. The road has been tough at times, but there is no one I would rather have been on that road with! My HERO! Love ya, Pop!

Index

Numbers in ***bold italics*** indicate pages with illustrations

Academy of Motion Picture Arts and Sciences (Academy Award or Oscar) 58, 88–89, ***96****–****97***, ***137***, ***146***
The Adventures of Tom Sawyer (film) 88
Akins, Claude 155–***156***
Alabama 104; Alabama International Motor Speedway 104; Talladega 104–***105***, 107, 110–***111***; Talladega 500 104; Winston 500 110
Alaska 168; Prince William Sound 168
Aldridge, Jesse 176
Aldridge, Robert 176
Aldridge, Taylor 176
Allen, Johnny 39, 72
Allison, Bobby (Allison) ***93***, ***105***, ***120***, ***129***
Allison, Donnie 88, ***122***
Ally McBeal (TV show) 144
American Automobile Association (AAA or Triple A) 13–15, 41; Big Car Division (Indianapolis) 15; Midget Division ***14***, 16–***18***, 20, 77, 131, ***135***, ***140***; Sprint Car Division 20, ***135***
Amos & Andrew (film) 154
Andretti, Mario 88
The Andy Griffith Show Reunion: Back to Mayberry (TV film) 154
Anheuser-Busch 44
Appalachian State University 2; Southern Motorsports (course) 2
Arkansas 27–28, 110, ***181***; LeHi 28; Memphis-Arkansas Speedway 28; Mid-South 250 28; Town Park Motel 27; West Memphis 27, 39, ***181***
Atlantic Ocean 30
Australia 85
Automobile Racing Club of America (ARCA) 86; ARCA 250 ***87***–88, 175

Bailey, H.B. 114
Baker, Buck (Buddy's father) 4, 15, ***23***, ***29***, 42, 48, ***55***–56, ***58***, ***65***–***66***, 68–70, 72–76, 79–82, 101, 108, 114–***115***, 173
Baker, Buddy ***23***, 69, 71, 79, ***96***, 108, ***129***–130, 173–***174***
Baker, Erwin George "Cannon Ball" 58
Baker, Margaret (Buck's wife) ***23***, 75–76, 98
Baker Equipment Company 106

Ballard, Walter ***111***–112
Bank of America 28, 119
Baretta (TV show) 143
Battleground (film) 58
Beam, Alex 20, 180; museum (Alex Beam's or Alex's) 20, 123, 145, ***179***
Beaumont, Charles 57
Beaumont, Harry ***96***, 97
Beck, Martin 153
Betters, Warren 180
Bixby, Bill ***94***
Black-ish (TV show) 144
Blanton, Charlie 118
Blazing Saddles (film) ***137***
Boger, Tommy 21
Bojangles 172
Bond, Julian ***137***
Bonnett, Neil 160–***161***
Boy Scouts ***9***
Boys Town (film) 88
Brady, Scott 156
Brickhouse, Richard ***105***
Bridges, Beau ***137***, ***153***
The Broadway Melody (film) 97
Brooks, Dick 108, ***122***, 130
Brotherton, Allen 171
Bruner, Johnny 26–27, 72, 82
Bruner, Mary ***11***
Budweiser 44
Buick 25, ***32***; Skylark 25
Burrs Lincoln Mercury 152

Cadillac 13, ***14***, ***29***, 36, 43, 124
Calhoun, Rory (Mitch Cooper) 50–***52***, ***55***, 155–***156***
California ***38***, 45, ***73***, ***120***, 132–133, 147, 159, 167; Hollywood 1, 3, ***58***, 60, 97, 130, 133, ***135***–136, 144, ***158***, 169; Los Angeles 167; Motor Trend 500 106; Riverside ***73***, ***105***–106, 133
Calley, Lt. William Laws ***109***–110
Campanella, Joseph 58
Can Am (racing series) ***122***
Canada 37; Niagara Falls 37; Ontario 37; Stamford Park 37
Car Wash (film) 143

Index

Castles, Chloe 176, 186
Castles, Donald Jackson (Neil's father; Grandfather Castles) 7–*10*, 20–21, 185
Castles (Wolfer), Donna (wife of Dean Wolfer) 113, 131, 176, *181–182*
Castles, Elizabeth Rucker (Neil's mother) 7–*10*, *19*–21, 34
Castles, Jean (Neil's wife; Mom) 3–4, *19*, 28–*29*, 34, 43–44, 64, 68, 75–76, 81, 84, 88, 98, 100, *117*, 130–133, 136, 139, 150, 152, 155, 157, 160–167, *170*, 172, 176, 178–*179*, *181–182*, 186; Alzheimer's program at Duke University 178
Castles, J. N. (Neil's grandfather; Grandpa) 7–9
Castles, Neil, Jr. 4, 145, 149, 155, *170*, 176, 178, *181–182*, 185
Castles, Susan (Mowbray; wife of Ken) *126*, 155, 175–176, *179*, *181–182*, 184–186
Castles, T-Bone (Angus bull pet) 124–*125*
Castles, Uncle Dave 21
Castles, Uncle Ed 8
Castles, Zac 176, 186
Castles Pit Stop Marina 160–*163*, *167*–168
CBS 57
Challenge (film) 150, 152–*153*
Champion, Bill (Champ) 37, *174*
Chevrolet (Chevy) *14*, 26, 43, *51–53*, 56, *58*, 68–69, 72, 81, 99, 119–121, 134, 142–144; Black Widow *58*; Blazer 145; Camaro 113, 131, 172, 186; Chevelle 82, 88, 99; Corvette 152–*153*; Howard/Castles Kmart/Pistonlube (racecar) *120*; Monte Carlo 120
Chicago (city) 44, 64–*66*
Chicago Hope (TV show) 144
Chick-fil-A 178
Childress, Richard 4, *129*–130, 133
Chrysler (300) 36, 65, 68–70, 72–*73*, 75–81, 86, *94*, 103, *105*–107, 127, 173, 175; hemi engine 82; Kiekhaefer Chrysler 36, 75; Winged Warriors *105*–106
Cloninger, Bob 166
Clooney, George (Clooney) 145
Coca-Cola 86
Colvin, Bob *14*, 37, 39, 48–*52*, 60–61, 84, *135*, 180
Colvin, Leland *14*–15, *18*, 22–*24*, 26–28, 30, 39, 44, *73*, *135*, 180
Combs, Roby *11*
Connecticut *74*, 107; Thompson 107
Connors, Paul 82
Converse, Frank *156*
Cooley High (TV show) 143
Cooper, Doug 75
Cooper, Jackie 88
Cozza, Mike 165
Cracker Barrel *154*
Crawford, Spook 39
Creach, Everett (Creach) 144–*146*, 180
Crider, Crawfish 30–*33*

Cromwell Helmets 20
Cushman Motorcycles 16–*17*

Davenport, Buddy 30, *32*, 34–35
Death at the Stock Races (TV show; aka *Death of a Race Driver* and *I, Buck Larsen*) 56, 136
Declarations of Stock Car Independents (book) 123, *177*
Delaware 138–139; Dover 138; Dover Speedway 138
DePaolo, Pete *38*–39; Pete DePaolo Engineering *38*
DeVault, Russ 114–*116*
DeWitt, L.G. 77, 118
Diamonds Are Forever (film) 144
Dickens, Bunny 100
Dickens, Neil 100, 113
Dieringer, Darel 41, 82–83
Dirty Harry (film) 144
District of Columbia *164*–165, 168; attorneys 165; Court of Appeals 166; Washington *164*, 167
Dodge 3, 27, 62, 64–65, 69, 72, *74*, 79, 82, 89, *93*, 98–99, 103, 106, 108–*109*, *111*, 118, 124, 127–*129*, 132–133, 144, 172, 175; Charger (500) *93*, 103, *105*, 107–*109*, *111*, *125*, 133, 172; Daytona (winged racecar) *105*, 107–108, *111*; *Dukes of Hazzard* car 172; Free Lt. Calley (racecar) 108, 110; Howard Furniture (racecar) 118; Super Bee *128*
Donovan, Brian 144
Duncan, Ted *140*
DuPont 15
Duray, Leon 97
Dye, Waco 16, *18*; D.B. Dye Bolt Company 16

Earnhardt, Dale, Jr. (Dale's son) 160, 173
Earnhardt, Ralph (Dale's father) 127, 160, 173
Earnhardt, Ralph Dale, Sr. (Dale) 127–*129*, 132–133, 160–*161*, 173
Edelbrock Heads 21
Elliott, Federal Judge J. Robert *109*
Emmy (TV award) *58*
England 30, *32*–35, 39, 41, *135*, 180; British Government 30; Harringay Arena 30–*31*; London 30; Scotland Yard *32*; Southampton *33*; World Championship Stock Car Races 30–*32*
Epton, Joe 26, 28–*29*, 98
espnW.com (auto racing website) 2
Eubanks, Joe 27, *181*
Exxon Corporation 3–4, *162*–168, 171–172, 183, 187; *Exxon Valdeze* (oil tanker) 168

Figari, Lou 75–76
Firestone (Tire Company) 142
Fish, Old Man 25; Fish Carburetor 24–25, 103
Flock, Fonty *40*–41

190

Index

Flock, Tim 36, 42, 46, 61
Florida 24, **29**, 45, 112; Beach and Road Course 45; Bold City 200 112; Days Inn 88; Daytona **19**, 22, **24**–25, 27, 44, 46, 64, **73**–**74**, 81, 86–88, 100, 103, **116**, 119–**120**, **125**; Daytona Beach **24**–25, **29**, 45, 47, **73**–**74**, **117**–118, 124; Daytona 500 **66**, 86–88, 108; Daytona International Speedway 74, **105**; Firecracker 400 **74**; Fish Carburetor **24**–25, 103; Fort Lauderdale 26; Governor 45; Halifax Hospital 63–64; Halifax River 25, 103; Hialeah 26; Jacksonville 71, 112; Jacksonville Speedway 112; Measured Mile **29**; Miami 26–27; Orlando 25; Speedway Park 71; Speed Weeks 88, **105**; Streamline Hotel (Ebony Room) 25; West Palm Beach 26
Folse, Pete 30, **32**–**33**
Ford (or Ford Motor Company) **11**, 13–15, 20, 22–**23**, 25, 28–**29**, 34, 36–39, 42–43, 45, **49**, **54**–56, **58**, 63, 66–67, 72–**73**, 77, 81, 99, **116**, 127, 136–139, 142, 145–**146**, 148, 173, 180; Café Burgundy Galaxie (racecar) 67; Explorer 148; flathead engine **14**, 25, **137**–138, **146**; Model A 12, 118, **148**–149; Model B 149; Model T (T-Model) 145–146, **148**, 176–**177**; modifieds 11, 13, 14, 20, 23, 73, 137; Mustang 127; overhead engine **38**; Police Interceptor **14**; six-cylinder business coupe **14**; Schwam Motors (Purple Fords) **34**–37; Thunderbird (T-Bird) 44, **148**; transmissions 22; warehouse 80
Fordillac 13
Fox, Ray 25, 72, 103–104
Foyt, A.J. 106
France, Annie 88
France, Bill, Jr. **87**–88
France, Bill, Sr. (France) 25, 27, 43, **49**, 61, 76, 88, 104, **115**–**116**, 119, 124, **126**, 180
Frank, Larry 67–69, 173; Go Kart shop 67–68
Frasson, Joe **129**
Frazier, Brother Bill 100–101
Friel, Norris 98

Gallion, Dennis **126**, 172
Gant, Harry 133
Garbo, Greta **96**
Gardenia, Vincent **137**
Gaskins, Mr. 167–168
Gazaway, Bill 98, **111**, 114
Gazaway, Joe 98
Gentlemen Prefer Blondes (film) 50
Georgia 43, **54**, 110, 138–139, 141, 155, **174**–175; American Fighting Man's Day 110; Athens 138–139; Athens Speedway (racetrack) 139–**140**; Atlanta 4, 16, 61, 68–69, **111**, 114, 118, 141, 145, 155, 175, 178; Atlanta General Motors 143; Atlanta International Raceway 114; Augusta 71; Carnesville 175; Governor Jimmy Carter 110; I-85 175; Macon 82, 141; Peach Bowl 61; penitentiary (jail) 141–142; Powers Ferry 175
Gibson, Mel **154**
Gilliam, Emory (Gil) 86–88; Gilliam Automotive 88
Gilligan's Island (TV show) 50, 134
Glotzbach, Charlie (Chargin' Charlie) 119–**120**
Gojo 187
Goldsmith, Paul 41–42, 62–63, 86, 103, **105**–107
Goodyear Tire and Rubber Company 106–107, 130, 142–143
Graham, Billy 30–**31**
Granger, Gene 130
Grant, Crash 142–143
Gray, Don 38
Gray, Henley 82
Greased Lightning (film) 2, 72, 136–**137**, **140**, 144, **146**, **153**–**154**, 176
The Green Berets (film) 144
Grey Rock 67
Grier, Pam (Mary Scott) **137**
Griffith, Andy Samuel (Andy) 147–**151**, 173
GT Motorsports (newspaper) 2
Gurney, Dan 106
Guy, Richard 101

Hagen, Ross (Paul Dado) **92**–**93**
Haines, William (Bill Whipple) **96**
Hale, Alan, Jr. 50–**51**, 134
Harb, Fred 56
Hard Driving (book) 144
Harkey, Bob 16, **18**
Harley Davidson **17**, 64, **66**
Harrah, Bill 149
Harris, Jo Ann **156**
Hartz, Harry 97
Havens, Richie **137**
Hawks, Howard 50
The Heist (film; alternate titles: *High Risk, Riders, $teal, Steal, Team Riders*) **156**, **158**
Hello, Dolly! (film) 50
Helmick, Paul 50
Helms, Jimmy 69–70, 72, 81
Hindman, Earl (Beau Wells) **137**, **140**
Hines, Connie 50–**51**, **55**
Hoffa, Jimmy 61
Holiday Inn 157–**158**
Hollywood Foreign Press Association (Golden Globes) 58, 137, **146**
Holman, John (salesman) 152
Holman, John (team owner) **38**, 68, 85, 152
Holman and Moody (Holman-Moody) 68–69, 72–**73**, 84–85, 99, 152
Home Fires Burning (book) 165
Home Improvement (TV show) **137**

Index

Hooters 149, *151*
Hot Summer in Barefoot County (film) 2, *109*
Householder, Ronnie 106
How the West Was Won (film) 144
How to Marry a Millionaire (film) 50
Howard, Richard 88–89, *93*, 101–104, 118–121, 127, *129*, 132–134, 180; Denver Equipment Company 118; Howard Furniture 118
Howard, Ron (Opie Taylor) *154*
Howco International Pictures 50
Huckleberry Finn (film) 88
Huggins, Ross 142
Hurtubise, Jim (Herk or Old Crispy) 88, 123–124
Hutcherson, Dick 96
Hylton, Evelyn 124, 175–176
Hylton, James Harvey (James) 101, 108, 124–*125*, 175–*177*
Hylton, James Harvey, Jr. (Tweety or the boy) 175–*177*
Hyman, Neil 147

Indian (motorcycles) *17*
Indiana *54*; Highland 106; Indianapolis 500 16, *38*–39, 97, 123; Kokomo *54*
Inman, Bob 165
Internet Movie Database (IMDb) 50, 57, *95*, 139, 144, 150, *156*, *158*
Irick, Bill 30
Isaac, Bobby 118, *122*, 134–*135*

Jackson, Maynard *137*
Japan 173–*174*; Suzuka Circuitland *174*; Suzuka City *174*
Jarrett, Ned 72
Jett, Dr. 155
Johns, Bobby 60, *105*
Johnson, Junior 67, 72, 119, 121, 172
Jones, Possum 30, *32*–33
Jones, Roy *19*, 25
Joseph, Mel 138

Kansas 110
Kelly, Dippo 12, 118
Kiser, Ike 67
Kite, Harold 81
Knox, Eddie 171

L.A. Law (TV show) 144
Langdon, Shep *38*
Langley, Elmo 107, *116*, 118, 173
Larson, Mel 43
The Last American Hero (film) 2, *153*
Leatherheads (film) 145
Lewellen, Jimmy 26
Lincoln (auto) 100, 147
Little, Cleavon 137
Littlejohn, Joe 118

Litz, Deacon 97
Livingston, Ed 72
Lockhart, Kyle *153*
Loftin, Carey (Tommy Webb) 50–*51*, *54*, *95*, 155–*156*, 180
Long, Bondy 15
Lund, Tiny 4, 42, *96*, 113, *122*, 184
Lynn, Clyde 81–82

MacDonald, Dave 123
Mafia 44
Maine *74*
Marcis, Dave 114, *122*
Marcum, John 86
Marlin, Coo Coo *122*
Martin and Lewis 88
Marty (film) 50
Maryland 107; Beltsville 107
Matlock (TV show) 147, *151*, 176
Mayne, Roy *96*
McDonald, Frank 57
McDuffie, J.D. 81
McDuffie, Paul 60
Mercury *38*, 41–42, 46, 56, 75; Marauder 75
Metro-Goldwyn-Mayer (MGM) 88–*91*, *96*–97, *122*
Michigan 13, 108, *120*; Berlin Speedway *120*; Brooklyn 108; Detroit 13; Marne *120*; Michigan International Speedway 108
Miller, Charlie 20
Miller, Don 149; Miller Racing Team 149
Miller, Nicky *137*–139
Miller Beer Company 149
Millstein, Cohen, Hausfield, and Toll (law firm) 168
Milwaukee 123
Mississippi 110; Mississippi River 27
Mr. Ed (TV show) 50
Mitchum, Robert 50; D.R.M. Productions 50
Moody, Ralph 61–62, 68, 72
Moore, Bud 43, 62, 64, 75, 130
Moore, Doug 75
Moore, Greg 4, 62
Morrow, Vic (Tommy Linden) *58*
Mountain Dew 187
Movin' On (TV show) 143, 155; *The Big Wheel* (episode) *156*; Red Banning (Neil's role in *The Big Wheel*) *156*
Mowbray, Ken (husband of Susan Castles) 176
My Friend Flicka (film) 144
My Life in Idlewild (film) 187
Myers, Chocolate 160
Myers, Billy *40*–41
Myers, Bob (journalist) 116
Myers, Bobby (racer) 30–*33*, *40*–41, *54*

192

Index

NAACP 76
Nab, Herb 119, 121*NASCAR Winston Cup Scene* (newspaper) 2
Nash 70
Nashville Network 175
National Association for Stock Car Auto Racing (NASCAR) 1, 5, *11*, 25–*29*, *31*, 37, *40*–41, 43, 47, 61, 67, 71, 72, 80, 82, 84, 86, 89, 97–99, 104–*105*, 108, 112–*117*, *120*, 122, 127, 130, 180, 183; awards ceremony *117*; Convertible Division (rag tops) 1, 37, 41, 43, 45–46, 61, *135*; Grand American Division 104, 112; Grand National Division 3, *14*, 27, 37, *40*–41, 43–45, 47, *54*–*55*, 67–68, *74*–75, 101, *105*, 107, 112, *135*, 142, 144, 173; Grand National East Division 1, 112–114, *116*, 118, 121–*122*, *129*, *135*; Hall of Fame 101, 134–*135*; Modified Division 11, 13, *14*, 20, 22, 25, 37, *73*, 131, *135*, *146*; Monster Energy Cup Series 75; Speedway Division 15, 37; Sportsman Division *129*, *135*; Strictly Stock Car Division 75; Winston Cup Series (Winston) *74*, 108, 112–113, *116*, 121–*122*, *129*, 133–*135*, *140*
Negre, Ed 132–133; wife 132
Negre, Norman 132–133
Nelson, Norm 88
New Jersey *74*–75, 110; Jersey City 75; Old Bridge 75
New Orleans 85–86
New York *29*, *33*, *49*, 75, 77–*78*, 101, 145, 149; Bridgehampton 75, *78*, 175; Bridgehampton Raceway *78*; Islip 77; Long Island 75, 77, 175; Malta 107; New York (City) *140*–141; Syracuse *29*, 47; Watkins Glen 75–77; Watkins Glen International Raceway 75; Woodstock (rock concert) *137*; Yellow Cabs 145
Nichels, Ray 69, 103, 106
North Carolina 1–3, 7–*10*, *14*, 16, *18*, 20–21, 27, 35–37, 39, 41–42, 44, 57, 100, 114, 118, 123, 133, 142, 147–*148*, 150–154, 156, *158*–159, *161*, *163*–*164*, 167, 171, 176, *179*–180, 183, 186; Asheville 2, 42, 48, 50, 71, 81, 101–*102*, *137*, *146*; Asheville Tourists 48; Asheville-Weaverville (Speedway) 42, 71; Bald Head Island 176; Barringer Drive 44; Belmont *102*; Biscuitville 118; Boiling Springs 150; Bowman Gray Stadium 41, *116*; Brevard 50; Burgaw *156*; Carolina 500 1, 134; Carolina Machine Shop 103; Charlotte 1, 3, 7, *9*–*10*, 22, *14*, *18*–*19*, 26, *33*–35, 37, 43–44, 63, 65, 67, 69, 72–*73*, 77, 81–82, 84, 86, 88–89, 104, 106–107, *111*, 119, 121, 123, *125*, *128*–131, 134, 152, 157, 160, 165; Charlotte (airport) *126*; Charlotte City Council 171; Charlotte Fairgrounds 131; Charlotte (hospital) 123; Charlotte Motor Speedway 61, 64, 66, 72, 81, *83*, *91*–*92*, 101, 106, *128*, 132, 134, 155; *Charlotte Observer* 58–59, 165; Cliftwood Street 12; Concord 27; Conover 44; Denver 118; Derita *9*; Dilworth *9*–*10*, 12; Fayetteville 39; Figure Eight Island *148*; Fort Bragg *10*; Gastonia 180; Gilkey 7, *9*; Graham Street *10*; Green Hill *9*; Greensboro 37, *111*, 142; Hickory 34–36; Hickory Speedway 36, *135*, 172; Highway Patrol 13; Highway 221 7–*8*, 150, 152; Hillsborough *58*, 80; Hillsborough Speedway 3, 56–57; Holy Angels Nursery *102*–103, 118; Home Depot 168; The Incentive Plan 159; Interstate 40 150; Interstate 70 152; Kannapolis 167; King's Mountain 16, *18*, 20; Lake Norman 160–*162*; Lenoir *9*; Lincoln Street *10*; Manteo Island 149; Marion 7, 100, 152; Mayberry 147; McCormick Field 48; McFarland (publishing company) *177*; Mecklenburg County 3; Merriman Avenue *9*; Midland 20–21; Monroe 21, *24*, 81–82; Mooresville 118, 123, 146, 149, *179*; Morehead Street 67; Mount Airy 147; Mount Holly *102*; Mountain Creek Baptist Church 7; NASCAR Hall of Fame (Hall of Fame) 28, 101, 134–*135*; National 400 81 (500) *129*; NCNB Bank 28; North Carolina Motor Speedway 134, *174*; North Carolina State Fairgrounds 107; North Tryon Street 67; North Wilkesboro (Wilkesboro) 47, 119, 172; Oakdale Road *163*; Occoneechee Speedway 57, 80; Park Road 72; Paw Creek 3, *162*–*164*, 166, 169–*170*, 172, *179*–180; Paw Creek Environmental Association (Investigations or Committee) *164*–165, 167–168; Pine Island Country Club 3, 171–172; Pineville *14*; Presbyterian Hospital 169–*170*; Raleigh 107, 114, 165–166; Raleigh Speedway *24*; Red Springs 42–43; R.J. Reynolds Tobacco Company 22, 108; Rockingham 1, 59, 113, 118, 134, 173–*174*; Rutherfordton 7; Shelby *11*, 20, 150, *153*; Southport *148*; Spruce Pine *8*; Starlite Speedway 81–82; Statesville Avenue 112; Sullins Road 64, 130–131, 152; Taylorsville 133; Thermal City 7, *9*; Union Mills *8*; Welcome 4; Wilmore Church 28; Wilmore Drive 68; Wilmore Food Store 12; Wilmore Presbyterian Church 60; Wilmore School 12; Wilmore Section *9*; Wilkinson Boulevard *38*, 79–80; Wilmington 118, *148*–149, *151*, *154*, 157, 167, 176, 178, 180, 186; Winston-Salem 22, 41, *73*, 114–*116*; World Service Life 300 127–*128*; World 600 (the 600) 3–4, 72, 82–*83*, *85*, 88, *91*–*92*, 97, 119–121, *129*, 132–134; Wray Frazier Camper Sales 118; Wrightsville Beach *148*, 183
Northern Tour *74*–78

Old Timers Racing Association 4
Oldsmobile (Olds) 4, *23*–*24*, 26–27, *40*, 44, *74*, *78*, 80, 82

Index

Oliver, Jackie *122*
Osiecki, Bob 64
Owens, Cotton (Cotton) 62–63, 65, 71, *73*, 89, *93*, 108, *111*, 127, 134, 173
Owens, Herman 13–*14*, 16
Owensby, Earl (The Dixie DeMille) 150–*151*, *153*; E.O. Corporation *153*

Packard (auto) *148*–149
Page, Anita (Pat Bonner) *96*, 97
Panch, Marvin 41–42, 45, *66*–67
Pantera (auto) 150, 152
Paschal, Jim 42
The Patriot (film) 145, *154*
Pearson, David 71, 104, 118, *122*; kids 113
Pembroke Indian 42
Pennsylvania 20, *38*, 41, 47, *74*, 157; Langhorne 20, *38*, 41–42, 47; Puke Hollow 41
Pepsi 43
Petillo, Kelly 39
Petty, Julian 43
Petty, Lee 27–28, *40*–41, 43, 56, 75
Petty, Maurice 101
Petty, Richard 56, 59, 72, 77, *93*, *95*, 104, 107–108, 114, *116*, 180; The Pettys 173
Picket Fences (TV show) 144
Picture Cars 144–145, 159, 180
Pires, Gerard *156*
Pistone, Tom (Tiger Tom) 44–45, *122*, *126*, *179*
Plymouth *74*, 82, 86–88, *93*, 127
Pontiac (auto; aka Iron Indian) 41, 43–44, 69
The Practice (TV show) 58
Presley, Elvis (Elvis or Steve Grayson) 1, 3, 79, 88–*90*, 92–*94*, *96*, *122*, 136
Professional Drivers Association (PDA) 104–*105*
Pryor, Richard 136–*140*
Pugh, Digger 30–*31*
Purcell, Pat 71
Putney, J.T. 71, 79, 81

Queen Elizabeth (ship) *33*–34
Queen Mary (ship) 30

RacinToday.com (auto racing website) 2
Reed, Jerry 145, *154*
Reed, Jim *55*
Reno (city) 149
Rhode Island 178; Newport 178
Rice, Kenneth *83*
Richter, Les 49
Ringling Brothers and Barnum and Bailey Circus 30
Rio Bravo (film) 50
River of No Return (film) 50
Robbins, Marty 124
Roberts, Doris 72–*73*

Roberts, Fireball 4, *11*, *14*, *18*–*19*, 22–25, 27, 39–*40*, 42, 56, *58*, 72–*73*, *181*
Robertson, T. Wayne *140*
Robinson, Ernest *140*
The Rockford Files (TV show) 143
Rogers, Kenny *146*, *154*-155
Rossi, Mario 44
Rupert Seat Belt Company 44
Rush, Ken 41
Russell, Harold 180

Sachs, Eddie 123
Sawyer, Paul 13, *120*
Schultz, Michael (Michael) 143
Schuyler, Bobby 30
Scott, Mary 72, 184
Scott, Wendell Oliver 72–*73*, 76–77, 82, 121–*122*, *137*–142, 144, 184; lawyer 141; son 141–142, 144
The Screen Actors Guild–American Federation of Television and Radio Artists (SAG) 50, 62, *146*–147; awards *146*–147; card *146*
Sears, John 77, 107
September 11, 2001 (9/11) 157–*158*
Sgt. Pepper's Lonely Hearts Club Band (film) 144Shepherd, Morgan *129*
She Wore a Yellow Ribbon (film) 144
Shockley, Bill *78*
Shuman, Buddy *10*–*14*, 16, 20–22, 27, 30, 34–38, 42, *73*, 108, 118, *135*, 180; Buddy Shuman Award 37
Shuman, Frank 35
Shuman and Thompson Garage (shop or university) *10*–13, 21–22, *24*, *33*
Silver Express (train) *33*
Sinatra, Nancy 88–89, *94*, *96*
Sister Teresa 103
Six Pack (film) 2, *146*, *154*-155, 175
Skeen, Buren 80–81
Skippy (film) 88
Smith, Jack 42, 72
Snow, Les 104
Soap Box Derby 1, *10*, 12, *18*, 118, 187
Soldier Field 44
Son of Shaft (film) 178
South Carolina 1, *14*, 16, 22–*23*, 45, *49*–*51*, 84, 108, 110, 113, 124, *126*, 145, 149; Camden *14*-15, 22–*23*, 27, *73*; Camden Military School *23*; Charleston 1, 37, 42, 45, 107–108, 110, *126*; Columbia Speedway 3, *73*, *109*–110, *126*; Darlington 1, *14*–15, 22–*23*, 37, 39, 47–*51*, 60, 65, 68, 70, 84, 101, 103–104, 123, 142; Darlington Motel *52*, 142; Darlington Raceway *14*, *49*, *51*–*52*, 80, 84; Darlington Stripe 70; Florence 60; Florence (hospital and The Bleeding Room) 60; Greenville 68, 113, 118, 149; Greenwood 22, 30; Hartsville 50, 84; Hartsville Speedway 50–*51*; Inman 124; Myrtle Beach 47; Rebel

194

Index

400 104; Southern 500 1, *23-24*, 37-41, 50, *54-55*, 60-61, 67-68, 80, 123; Spartanburg 7, 20, 27, 65, 68-69, 79, 113, 124-*125*, 127, 130, 145, 173; *Spartanburg Herald* 47; White Horse Road 68
Southern Automotive Journal (newspaper) *116*
Speedway (1968 film) 1, 3, 88-89, *91-94*, 96-97, 136; (1929 film) *96-97*
Spence, Bill 97
Spencer, G.C. *96*, 121-*122*, *140*
Staley, Enoch 47
Staley, Gwyn 42, 46
Stansell, Chuck 64-*66*
Starsky and Hutch (TV show) 143
Step, Bill 62, 68, 101
Strickler, Bub 48
Stroppe, Bill *38*, 42, 46
Studebaker 187
Stunt Coordinator *140*, 144, *146*
Stunt Double *140*
Stunt Driver *140*
Stunt Man (stunting) *155*, 169, 180
The Summer of Ben Tyler (film) *156*
Sweatlund, Charles 60
Swinson's Food Products 12

Taurog, Norman 88-89, *94*
Taylor, Doc (doctor) 169
Taylor, Mr. (Joe) 60
Taylor, Pete 103
Teamsters Union (Teamsters) 61-62, *146*
Tennessee 34, 107, 113-114, 118, 121, *125*, 144; Bristol 121, *125*; Maryville 107, 113-114, 118; Nashville 34, 100, 107, 113, 124, *154*; Smoky Mountain Raceway 114; Volunteer 500 121
Texaco 22
Texas 110, 167, 173, 176, 186; Houston 176, 186; Spring 183
Third World Cinema *137*
Thomas, Herb 41
Thomas, Jabe 107
Thompson, Bruce 21
Thompson, Jimmy 21
Thompson, Speedy *14*-15, 21, *23*, 25, 39, 42, 56-57, 68, 131
Thompson, Willie *10*-13, 20-22, 34, *38*, 98, 180
Thunder in Carolina (film) 3, 50-*53*, *55*-56, 134, 136, 142, 155
Thunder Road (film) 1-2, 136
To Have and Have Not (film) 50
Tora! Tora! Tora! (film) 144
Touched by an Angel (TV show) 144
The Towering Inferno (film) 144
Transportation Coordinator (transportation) 144-*146*
Turner, Curtis 34, 36-*38*, *52*, 61-62, 81; Curtis Turner Achievement Award 121

Tyner, Roy (The Wild Indian or Private Indian) 42-44, 60, *94-95*, 103; Cousin Vern 43

Union Oil (Pure Oil) *23-24*, 80, *154*; Peggy 80; Smitty 80
United Artists 50
United States (USA) *33*, 157, 184; Federal Judge J. Robert Elliott *109*; House of Representatives 110; President Richard Nixon 110; White House 110
U.S. Air Force (Air Force) 43, 124
U.S. Army (Army) *9-10*, 16-*17*, 21, 81, *109*, *177*
Universal Studios 134
Utah 110

Vanadore, Lester 30, *32*, 34-36
Vandiver, Jim *105*, 123, *129*-130, 144, *156*; wife 123
Vanishing Point (film) *137*
Van Peebles, Melvin (Melvin) 136, 138-139, 141, 143
Van Sickel, Dale 50
Vietnam *109*; My Lai Massacre *109*-110; Viet Cong 110; War *109*
Virginia 2, *17*-18, 21, 46, 82, 166; Court of Appeals 166; Greasy Corners *17*-18; Hampton 82, 107; Joe Weatherly 150 80; Martinsville 121; Norfolk *17*-18, 21; Norfolk Hospital 21; Richmond 13, 45-46, 82, 107, 166; Richmond Memorial Hospital 47; Richmond Speedway *120*; Strawberry Hill 13, *17*
Vogt, Red *24*-25

Wade, Billy 75
The Walker Agency 89
Wallace, Governor George 110
The Waltons (TV show) 145
Warner Brothers *137*
WBT-TV 165-166
Weatherly, Joe 4, 34, 36-37, 43, *52*
Welborn, Bob 43, 47
West Virginia 108, 157-*158*; Charleston 157; Fayetteville *156*, *158*; New River Gorge Bridge *156*, *158*; Ona 108; West Virginia 300 108
What Comes Around (film) 2, 144, *154*
Which Way Is Up? (film) 144
White, Gene (Gene) 142; distributorship 142
Whitmore, James (Buck Larsen) 57
Widenhouse, Bill (Slab) 20-21, 25-27, 70
Wikipedia (online encyclopedia) *109*-110
Williams, Deb 1-2
Williams, Raymond (Captain America) 123
Winnebago 100
With God You're Always a Winner (book) 101
The Wizard of Oz (film) 88

195

Index

Wolfer, Dean (husband of Donna Castles) 176, 186
Wood, Glen 42
Wood, Perry Allen *179*
World War II *10*, 30, *177*; German prisoners *10*; halftrack (armored vehicle) *177*

Yarborough, Cale **96**
Yarbrough, LeeRoy 118
Young Guns (film) 144
Young Tom Edison (film) 88
Yunick, Smokey 25–26, 99

Zervakis, Emanuel 41